C000149025

# IT IS NOT SO EASY TO LIVE

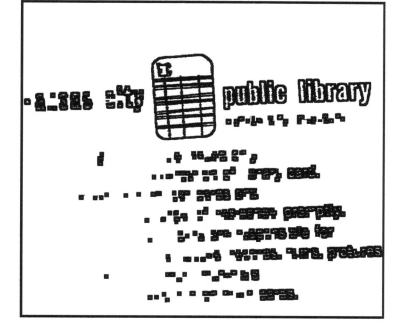

*It is not so easy to live*

BY CHRISTINE ARNOTHY

I AM FIFTEEN AND I DON'T WANT TO DIE
GOD IS LATE
THE CHARLATAN
I'S NOT SO EASY TO LIVE

# *It is not so easy to live*

CHRISTINE ARNOTHY

*Translated from the French by*
ANTONIA WHITE

E. P. DUTTON & CO., INC.
*New York*
1960

First printed in the U.S.A., 1960
by E. P. Dutton & Co., Inc.

Copyright, ©, 1958 in the English Translation
by Wm. Collins Sons and Co. Ltd., London

All rights reserved. Printed in the U.S.A.

¶ No part of this book may be reproduced in any form without
permission in writing from the publisher, except by a reviewer
who wishes to quote brief passages in connection with a review
written for inclusion in a magazine, newspaper or broadcast.

First published in French as *Il n'est pas si facile de vivre*
French edition ©, 1957, Librairie Artheme Fayard


Library of Congress Catalog Card Number: 60-7694

*To Claude*

# I

AFTER THE siege of Budapest, we had nothing left. The shells had made great holes in the front wall. I could have sat on our parquet floor, once so beautifully kept, and swung my legs out into empty space. The big house, divided up into flats, where I had spent fifteen years of my life had become a public danger. When the situation in Budapest had become stabilised and there were no longer any corpses in the streets, passers-by stepped off the pavement in front of our house and gave it a wide berth so as to avoid the risk of being crushed to death if it collapsed. The walls of my bedroom were full of cracks and those great black fissures affected me like open wounds.

We had not been able to save so much as a single object. The ruined remains of our old life were covered with an obscene deposit of filth. The vast rising tide of that bloody siege had withdrawn but it seemed to have left the city dirty for ever.

My mother's aunt used to wear a rose in her hair when she was young, but no photo of her survives. The only coffin she had was a pile of bricks and a mass of splintered glass. Towards the end of the war, the house where she lived collapsed on the tenants.

7

My aunt—I always called her that—was sixty-five and my uncle seventy, when I myself was six. I was a late arrival and only knew my grandparents from their photographs. On All Souls' Day, I used to be frightened when my parents took me to the cemetery. The sickly smell of the chrysanthemums, the little glass lamps, with their flickering flames, that everyone carried in their hands, filled me with inexplicable terror. For nights afterwards, I used to dream of ghosts and shiver under my blankets.

At seven, it seemed to me that everyone about me was old. I used to look long and thoughtfully at my mother's crow's feet and my father's greying hair.

My uncle and aunt lived on a fairly large pension. Their flat, on the gently-rising heights of Buda, was full of souvenirs of their travels. They had never had any children. I often used to spend the week-end with them. A little room was always kept ready for me. I can see my bed again now, and also a huge cupboard full of sheets, slightly yellow with age, tied up with broad red silk ribbons. Between the folds, my aunt had put lavender sachets; for a long time, my childhood dreams were impregnated with that mysterious scent.

Number 3, Rue Notre Dame; that was their address. My aunt, who always dressed in black, could never look at the plate that bore the name of the street other than with a hostile eye. She had once been deeply wounded in the confessional and, ever since, her resentment had included the entire priesthood. Very much later, I learnt that, as my uncle had been divorced, she had not been able to have a religious marriage. Carried away by the fervour of a great love, my aunt would have liked to have had the Church as an ally and so secure both earthly happiness and the blessing of Heaven. But instead of a blessing, she had been given an ultimatum and ordered to leave the man she loved.

In the hothouse of my childhood, I was, at any rate, carefully shielded from all the misfortunes that overwhelm grown-up people. My parents were kind and indulgent and, in my aunt's home, I learnt to love old people.

At eight years old, I was precocious enough to feel the depth of their love for each other in their looks and their gestures. They had a maid who was perfect in every respect, but it was always my aunt who helped my uncle on with his coat when he took me out for a walk. She would wait on the balcony till we emerged below into the street and her eyes would continue to follow us as we climbed the zigzag road. My uncle had a moustache that was beautifully groomed, though a trifle yellowed by the smoke of his eternal pipes. Dressed in black and carrying an elegant cane, he would stop at the turnings and explain to me that I must pay attention and give my whole mind to it. I would listen virtuously but I was enchanted when my hoop or my ball bounded away into the road and I had to make a breathless dash to retrieve them.

The Rue Notre Dame was lined with chestnut-trees. In the spring, their flowers scented the air; in the autumn, the ground was strewn with their prickly husks with the chestnuts bursting out of them.

After lunch, my uncle and aunt used to lie down; my aunt in her blue bedroom; my uncle on the sofa in the study, with his grey cape over him. During that time, curled up still and silent in my arm-chair, I would read Dickens. In those early afternoons, I made the acquaintance of David Copperfield and Mr. Pickwick. The maid went about three; Saturday was her free day. She would shut the front door so softly that I was the only person who heard the little click. Once I went out on to the balcony on tiptoe to watch her go. There was a soldier in front of the house. They went off together, hand-in-hand, and, suddenly, the drowsing flat seemed to me empty.

After dinner, if it was fine, my uncle and aunt would play cards on the balcony. The scarlet geraniums, with their velvety leaves, gave out a moist, peppery smell. Insects from all the nearby gardens came flocking round my aunt's opalescent glass lamp. When the old people played cards, they always spoke English. I would listen, half-asleep, to the sound of their conversation and the rustle of the cards.

On Sunday mornings, my father came to fetch me and then he and I and Mother would go to church. My aunt always shut the windows; she detested the sound of the Sunday bells. All the morning of that day, she used to play the piano. Now and then, my uncle, in his study, would hum the melody she was playing.

My aunt had a small private fortune; my uncle had nothing but his pension. But he possessed numerous greedy relatives whose visits my aunt, who was well-born and a trifle arrogant, regarded with extreme disfavour. Another thing depressed her; my confirmed hostility to the piano. Her long, silky fingers would fly lightly over the keys of her Steinway; when she played Chopin, my uncle would seat himself in an arm-chair and watch her.

For my tenth birthday, they made me a present of three books. One in Hungarian; the other two in English. What a birthday luncheon that was! My aunt had made some delicious ice-cream for me herself. While she and my uncle were taking their siesta, I looked at my beautiful books. As my arm-chair was close to my uncle's sofa, I could watch him as he slept. His large hands, dry and wrinkled as parchment, rested on his grey cape. On his right hand, he had a large wedding-ring; on his left, a heavy signet. I saw, from his watch, that it was ten minutes past four. I could hear my aunt's muffled footsteps as she got the tea ready in the drawing-room. I knew that, in a few minutes, she would come in and wake my uncle, and we should all have tea together. It would be a specially gay tea-party—and I should be able to finish the ice-cream from my festive lunch. Suddenly, it struck me that, on such an important occasion as my

11

birthday, I had a perfect right to wake my uncle up. So I slid out of my chair, and, without taking my eyes off him, touched his hand. But he was sleeping deeply, with his face turned to the wall on which hung an oriental carpet. The water for the tea was boiling. That made me more audacious still; I lifted the hand that wore the signet-ring. Warm, and incredibly heavy, it slipped out of mine and fell back, inert. My heart began to beat so violently that each beat hurt me like a stab.

"Uncle! . . . Uncle! . . ."

I must have screamed, for, the next moment, my aunt appeared in the doorway.

She had never seemed so tall and so slender as she did in that wintry twilight. I had the impression that she would never be able to enter the study. She looked at her husband and began to call him in a metallic voice:

"Darling, won't you come and have tea? . . . Tea, darling!"

A minute or two later, she sat down beside him and took the hand that had dropped from mine between her own hands.

"What have you done?" she asked. "How could you do that to me? Why didn't you wait to say good-bye to me? . . . You promised you would never go without saying good-bye to me. . . ."

I did not dare move. But it seemed to me that my uncle's lips had parted a little, as if for a last farewell.

12

My aunt began to move about with jerky, feverish gestures. She went into the bedroom, brought back a blanket and spread it over my uncle. Then she tried to telephone. But her fingers were trembling so much that she could not dial the number.

" Tell your parents to come over," she said to me. I telephoned.

While I was talking to my mother, my aunt turned on all the lights in the flat.

Suddenly, I was seized with a violent nausea. In winter, the geraniums from the balcony were kept indoors in the dining-room and their sickening smell filled the entire flat. I wanted to open a window but I could not manage to turn the handle. Why had my parents not arrived yet?

My aunt wandered from room to room muttering incoherent words about the tea and about death. The crude light left my uncle's face naked of all shadow. The face that had been animated only that morning had turned smooth and yellow before my eyes. His wrinkles had vanished and the grey moustache looked strangely incongruous on those features that now seemed ageless.

Now I could imagine that even my uncle had, once upon a time, been young.

The door-bell rang. I ran to the door and flung myself into my mother's arms. As I smelt the faint scent of her shoulder, I burst into sobs. I would have liked to stay there for ever, with my eyes shut, hidden in her arms.

So my uncle had gone away, before my eyes, into eternity. " You must always pay attention and give your whole mind to it," he used to say. But where was the elusive soul? I wondered. Where were his thoughts? Had he been dreaming before he died? What was there he might still have wanted to explain?

When I kissed his hand, it was already cold and lay crossed over the other on his breast.

After my uncle's funeral, I received a letter from my aunt. The black-bordered sheet was covered with her round, well-balanced handwriting.

" Dearest child," she wrote, " I want you to know that when I too am dead, like your uncle, all my possessions will belong to you. I should like you to keep the piano in the room you will have when you are a big girl. . . ."

I often went back to see her. The table was always laid for my uncle and the bottle of choice wine set beside his place.

The piano—she never played it again—remained silent and menacing in the middle of the big drawing-room. Like a coffin.

The last time I went into our own looted flat with my parents, I found something under some soiled books whose covers had been wrenched off. It was an engraving, almost undamaged in its frame, that showed the hill of Buda as it was at the beginning of 1900. Then I ventured into our dining-room that looked out on to the Fö-utca. I noticed a nail sticking out of the wall and I hung the engraving up on it.

Before our final departure, we stood for a moment in the street and looked up at our home for the last time. Through the gutted façade we could still see the engraving hanging up almost over empty space. Suddenly a brutal, impatient wind got up, scattering the grey dust. At that, we went away, our eyes full of ashes and tears.

In the little house of Fonyod, where I lived the life of a somnambulist, my one concern was to appear the typical growing girl who soon forgets troubles. I wanted to make things easier for my parents. I used to sing about the house to give them pleasure. With my mother's help, I cut myself out a summer dress from a flowered curtain. When my father said that everything was easier for the young, I agreed with him. In exchange for a pair of sheets, I managed to procure them a she-goat. The wrinkled peasant-woman who agreed to this barter taught me to milk her. The she-goat, who was old and good-natured, allowed me to.

But, at night, in my bedroom, I was restored to my true self; I dropped my mask of gaiety and returned to my books. Here, in the country, we had only some works by Scandinavian writers, a few Balzacs and one single Flaubert—*Madame Bovary*. My dreams were fantastic rides through a land of nightmares. Mademoiselle Julie was for me a dubious, almost treacherous friend. Sigrid Undset soaked me in an atmosphere of resigned melancholy that I found unbearable; once, when I was ill and feverish, I believed I was Ibsen's wild duck.

Pista, that young soldier who had been killed during the siege, often reappeared to me. But I was not frightened of him. Neither of him nor of my uncle. The peaceful death of an old man was, somehow or other, connected in my mind with the brutal death of a young one who had been bold and gay.

Every morning, life began afresh. The summers stretched out, stifling and interminable; the winters were rigid under the snow.

I remember one particular day in July. I had gone down to swim. The lake of Balaton carried me on its gilded blue back. Sometimes, looking behind me, I could see the dark green tracks ploughed up in the still water by my swimming. Human beings were so far away from me that I had the impression of being utterly alone. As I went on swimming, I raised my head, as if to discover the invisible God. Suddenly, an unexpected wave slapped against my face. And that little wet smack of sunlit water struck through me like an electric shock. All at once, I became, for the first time, aware of my own body.

In one shiver, I became aware of the very movements I was making in swimming. Clumsy and frightened, I made sure that my schoolgirl's bathing-dress covered my just-developing breasts.

Almost completely out of breath, I hurriedly turned back towards the shore. I had become heavy with exhaustion and, in a moment of inadvertence, I swallowed a great mouthful of water.

At last, feeling the pebbles under my feet, I collapsed on the shore.

I was breathing violently, almost passionately.

A little later, as I climbed up to the house again, I knew that my loneliness had become intolerable.

# 2

My ARRIVAL in Vienna had produced no impression on anyone. . . . We walked through the streets, less conscious of the torrential rain than of the cruel stare of the waiter in the café which had revealed that the Austrian schillings we had bought from our guide were worthless. Mamma had left him her last ring and now, urged on by fear, we were almost running, but with no idea of our destination.

At every turning, I expected to find some man or woman, with a kind smile, who would take us by the arm, conduct us into a warm room and then, with a discreet gesture, indicate the door of the bathroom to us.

Scrutinising the faces of the passers-by, I could discover nothing but dull eyes and drawn features; all those gazes seemed to me to run over us like the raindrops.

" Suppose we go back to the station? " said my father.

" And take a train? Where to? " asked my mother.

" There's a hostel for refugees there. A Station Hostel. We'll sleep there to-night and, to-morrow, I'll organise something."

As we had no money for a tram, we returned to the station on foot. There, we had to wait for my father while he went into the little office. I can still see that ruined station. Mamma was leaning back against a peeling wall: she looked so frail and vulnerable in this hostile dusk that I emerged from my little private world of dreams and vain expectation and kissed her thin face. She looked up at me with her blue eyes and smiled.

" The beginning of a new life is always very difficult, child. . . . But we are free."

Papa was a long time coming. I looked at my mother's swollen legs; her slender ankles were now a shapeless, painful mass of flesh. And nowhere, in all that deserted station, was there so much as a bench on which to sit down. Beside us, the door of a waiting-room swung open of its own accord, but the room had no roof to it. An occasional plate-layer, with hunched shoulders, passed by us without paying any attention. I knelt down in front of Mamma and laid my hand on one of her legs; it was burning hot.

" Are you in great pain ? "

" A little. . . ."

I had to make a great effort not to doze off. I could have gone to sleep then and there at Mamma's feet. Suddenly, as if they had sprung up out of the stone platform, we were surrounded by a crowd of passengers who were waiting for a train not yet signalled. I stood up. But I would have searched in vain for the faintest glimmer of interest in their eyes. I touched my own arm and ran my dirty fingers over my face. I wondered uneasily:

"Are we still visible? Perhaps we became transparent in that chilly moonlight? Perhaps our crossing the frontier was only a dream and I shall wake up at Fonyod again? . . ."

A harsh voice shouted: "*Barisnya burzsuj!*"

A huge Russian soldier had planted himself in front of us and was already pulling at my mother's fur coat.

The Russian made a sign to another soldier, pointed to my mother and kept repeating words we did not understand.

At that moment, Papa came back and told us to follow him.

We hurried after him, trembling, for the Russians were on our heels.

"I've just discovered that we are in the Russian zone," said my father.

We followed him, white with terror.

At last, we were able to go back into the barrack-like building.

A man with greying hair was waiting for us.

"Come this way. . . ."

The Russians remained outside.

We stumbled the whole length of a dark corridor and eventually arrived in a big room, lit by a single electric-light bulb. Then, at last, the man spoke to us:

"Of all the mad things to do! You cross the frontier illicitly and you go and gad about without papers in the Russian zone! Why didn't you go to the American zone or the French one?"

"The last time I came to Vienna—in 1926—I stayed at the Hotel Sacher," replied my father, his face livid with weariness. "How can you expect me to know the zones?"

The warden of the hostel, a colourless, melancholy person, promptly began to smile. The evocation of the Vienna of other days had a magical effect on him.

"Obviously! The Sacher. . . . But times have changed. . . . Stay here till to-morrow morning. . . . At eight o'clock sharp, I will take you to the frontier of the zone. There you can sort things out with the Reception Centre; it deals with refugees' papers."

In this great wooden room, rotten with rain, there were three long tables with benches along either side; the stove in the corner was heated red-hot.

"Sit down; they'll bring you some soup and some bread. The woman who will bring it must know nothing. If she asks any questions, tell her you've missed your train and haven't enough money to go to an hotel. Above all, don't undress in the dormitory. Here, in the Russian zone, there are any number of down-and-outs. Those are our night customers. . . ."

Unexpectedly, he held out his hand.

"Good night and good luck. . . . I'll see you again to-morrow morning."

We sat down on a bench. A few minutes later, the sweat was trickling all down our backs. Mamma and I were wearing at least three dresses apiece and Papa had five shirts on. While we were still in Hungary the guide had stopped us from taking a suitcase. So we had put on all our clothes, one on top of the other, and, for three days, we had never had a chance of undressing.

" At least, let us take off our coats," suggested Papa.

" No. The woman who brings the soup will see at once that we are wearing an abnormal amount of clothes."

So we waited, continuing to perspire.

She soon arrived. She was in her forties. Her greasy chignon clung to the nape of her neck like a bird's nest. She set a battered tray and three bowls of lentil soup before us, examining us with curiosity as she did so.

" Bread as well? " she asked.

Mamma nodded her head without saying a word.

The woman brought three pieces of bread.

With her shoulders drooped and her gaze riveted on us, she sat down beside the stove. I expected to see her melt in that heat like a candle. As I ate my warm soup, I had the crazy idea that, if I had a long arm and an extinguisher at the end of it, I could put her out! I returned her stare insolently. When the soup was finished, a grey deposit remained at the bottom of our bowls. The bread stuck to one's palate and tasted of clay. When the woman saw that we had really finished with our spoons, she beckoned to us to follow her.

Stuffed out with clothes under our heavy coats and stiff as scarecrows, we filed out after her.

At the door of the dormitory she left us and was swallowed up in dark corridors. The atmosphere of the dormitory was thick and smelt as if stuffed with garlic; a blue light hovered in a corner, filtering through a sort of fog. Those feeble rays from a single bulb dimly lit up heaps of dark rags. These were the sleepers, wrapped in their verminous over-coats. This vast twenty-fifth class sleeping-compartment possessed two rows of bunks. In the twilight, the top row seemed to me almost entirely empty; the passengers were clustered together in the lower one. We stepped forward cautiously but every breath made us swallow a mouthful of that stinking air that tasted like mud.

After occasionally knocking ourselves against the wooden scaffolding we finally found two empty places in the lower tier and one in the upper.

Mamma took off her coat and sat down on the edge of one of the beds. Papa stood there, his hat in his hand, completely bewildered. He was amazed that we should be free yet shocked and disillusioned, in spite of himself, by all these sordid details. Eventually, he lay down in the lower tier and I climbed up to the place in the upper one.

Our moving about had caused trouble among the sleepers. I could hear muffled voices. Over the edge of my extremely uncomfortable nest, I suddenly saw the face of a bearded man looking up at me from below.

His eyes glittered in the blue dusk; he was like an animal looking hungrily at a piece of meat. I drew back quickly and heaped the rough blankets over me. They smelt of suet; a cold, degraded wartime smell.

My skin was itching. I had the feeling of being devoured by a multitude of greedy, famished insects. I even thought I could feel the pricking of two sharp pincers on my knee. I felt about, with nervous disgust, but could find nothing.

All night long I was the prey of those imaginary insects. I economised my breath and only drew in tiny, prudent sips of air.

When we woke up, the dormitory was already empty. Heavy and drowsy from our suffocating night, we spoke very little.

In the big room, they gave us some more lentil soup; then the little man with the greying hair reappeared. His face was fresh and clean. He still had a dab of shaving-cream under one ear.

He gave my father an extremely useful address.

He spoke of his aunt who had a house in the American zone and who let rooms to refugees who had no papers but who were trustworthy.

The little man then took us to the limit of the Russian zone. It was a little street like any other; the cool morning wind had dried its pavements. Under the plate bearing the street's name was a placard: " Beginning of the American Zone."

Papa said good-bye to him; we all shook hands with him and he went away.

25

"He's a good sort," said Papa. "Yesterday, when I told him about all our bad luck, he lent me twenty schillings. Now we can go somewhere and have a hot drink in peace."

We went into a café in the Burgstrasse, the proprietress was still in process of sprinkling water on the dusty floor and sweeping it. Nevertheless she made us sit down and, a few minutes later, brought us the coffee.

I was delighted to know that we had twenty schillings.

" I'll leave you two here," said Papa. " I'll go to the Refugees' Reception Centre on my own."

I went out with him and he brought me a morning paper. Then I returned to Mamma. We were both prepared for a long wait. Before I had said good-bye to my father, a vague idea had occurred to me.

" How could he possibly have lent you money? " I asked him. " Was he so sure that you would come back."

Papa had frowned a little.

" Of course he was sure, since he had my promise. And, besides, I showed him all our schillings. He was horrified at our situation. These schillings are no longer current; they were withdrawn from circulation over a year ago. He has kept them. He is going to a bank to see whether he can get something for them. He might be able to, as he is Austrian. Of his own accord, he gave me twenty new schillings for these two thousand out-of-date ones."

I felt a rush of warmth and affection as I looked at my dear Papa who was so honest, so bound by the rules of a peaceful, bourgeois society that he was quite incapable of wondering even for one second, whether this distinguished down-and-out might not have cheated him.

Mamma and I read the paper. The proprietress of the café was very friendly. Mamma told her that we had crossed the frontier two days ago. She could speak freely; we were in the American zone. The good woman brought us four slices of bread on which she had spread a very little margarine—so little, you could hardly see it.

At a quarter to twelve Papa returned. We went off together to the Kleeblattgasse. At last, we were able to take a tram. Sitting just behind the driver, I saw my face, for the first time for three days, in his driving-mirror. I was incredibly ugly and my tears during the night had turned me into an Indian squaw, rather pale, but decidedly warlike. A tall, fair, very young man was sitting beside me. His presence seemed to me like a challenge to death. I had seen so many dead young men in the streets of Budapest! I was already imagining him lying stiff and still in a ragged uniform when he gave me a shy, friendly, almost frightened smile. Yes, he was alive, and so was I! But why was he smiling? Because I was ridiculous, unhappy, untidy and as heavy as a tortoise in my carapace of clothes? Or perhaps because I was twenty? I smiled too and turned my head towards the driving-mirror where I could see myself smiling. I wanted to say good morning to myself, too.

" We get off at the next stop," said Papa.

Almost as soon as we stood on the pavement, we were struck by the sunshine and the blue of the sky. It was a little depressed, that sun, intimidated by the month of November. But its feeble rays were glimmering on a strange world—a living world.

Vienna was at last welcoming us. What was that city just then? A vast birthday-cake cut into four slices; each of the four great Powers eating its own. Like ants who risked, at any moment, being crushed under the huge soles of army boots, the Viennese carried off only the crumbs of a former life.

I gave a little cry:

" Look, Mamma. . . ."

For the first time, in my life, I had just seen a black man. He was in uniform. My innocent astonishment had not escaped him; he smiled at me. It was the second smile of the day.

" Don't make any remarks," advised my mother. " Look, but don't say anything."

We arrived in the Kleeblattgasse. It was a little old street, just near the Graben. We stopped in front of an ugly, but dignified house, with thick walls. Papa pulled the bell and we heard the sound echoing and drifting through the house. No one came. Mamma pulled the bell, in her turn, and the clamour started up again, ricocheting back from the well of the stairs.

The door opened at last. A dark-complexioned man was standing on the threshold. Papa put his question:

" Is Madame Wagner in? We have been sent by her nephew. . . ."

The man told us to come in.

The hall was dark and the ancient staircase creaked under our feet.

A woman came to meet us and made us sit down in a bright, warm kitchen on the first floor. Papa explained to her that we needed a room for a few weeks and that we should soon be leaving for Innsbruck.

The first thing she mentioned was money.

" Have you any money? "

" Yes."

" How much? "

" How much are you asking for the room? "

" You haven't any papers? "

" Not yet."

She shrugged her shoulders.

" The risks are very considerable, here in Vienna. . . ."

" How much a day? " my father went on, with gentle tenacity.

She named the sum.

Papa made a small, lightning calculation and said, " Yes."

Having received two weeks' rent in advance, Madame Wagner took us up to the third floor, opened a door and left the key in the lock.

" There's running water, too. . . ."

Papa asked for some soap.  She promised to give us a piece.

The narrow room contained two beds, a cupboard and a wash-basin.  Without waiting a moment, we began to undress ourselves.  At record speed, I tore off, one by one, my crumpled frocks and my jumpers that were damp with perspiration.

What a deliverance!  But now the little room, with all our clothes in disorder, looked like a jumble sale.  On the beds, dresses were mixed up, higgledy-piggledy, with Papa's shirts.  Papa, standing, stripped to the waist, in the middle of the room was hunting for something.

" My hat was vanished," he said.  " Haven't you seen it, darling? "

" Do you need it at this moment? "

" No," replied Papa.  " But, all the same, I'd like to know where my hat is."

In the pocket of my winter coat, I found one of my high-heeled shoes.  But where was the other?

" You haven't seen my other shoe? "

" No," said Mamma, who had become slim and frail again.

" What are we going to do with all this stuff? "

" We'll have to buy a suitcase," said Papa, pouring water over his shoulders.

Madame Wagner brought us the soap.  Mamma opened the door just wide enough to let her in.

Soon the room was full of water and soapsuds.

Clean at last and wearing only the clothes we needed, we were aware of being ravenously hungry.

"We'll go and eat . . . and we'll buy a suitcase to put all these clothes in," said Papa.

Out in the street, he added:

"But we won't buy the suitcase in the Russian zone. The journey would end in Siberia."

It was half-past four. Already, the first lights of Vienna were beginning to wink. We had enough money for a small dinner. As we left the house, we noticed that not one of its windows was lit up. The little street hushed down in the darkness on its secrets and on our hopes.

While my parents were searching for their old Vienna, dressed up and mannered and peaceful; full of smiles and waltzes and the good smell of its famous coffee, I was looking avidly and excitedly at the Vienna of the present.

For Papa and Mamma, the city was a great actress, playing her last part. When her admirers came a little too close, she held a lace fan in front of her face to hide her deep wrinkles. But her voice, though slightly broken and hoarse from the smoke of the war, was still recognisable. It was a voice that went straight to the heart of those who had known genuine peacetimes and journeys without passports. . . .

What I saw was a Vienna full of soldiers of four nationalities, of badly-dressed people who were always shivering under the sleet, of shop windows that were brilliantly lit-up but almost empty. And I noticed how everyone was always in a feverish hurry to get back to their own homes.

When we left the Graben, we came to the Herrengasse. Mamma saw a church that was lit up inside.

"Let's go in," she said.

We made our way towards the wide-open door.

On the pavement, a Salvation Army woman was singing. Her voice seemed to defy the ample harmonies of the organ. We looked into the interior of the church. The aisle blazed in the yellow, quivering light of the tall candles. In the distance, the priest was celebrating the afternoon Mass and you could see his gold-embroidered chasuble. The tabernacle reflected the light so brilliantly that we could see the glitter of its metal door from where we stood in the street.

I was seized with an inexplicable feeling of discomfort. The little woman in blue went on singing and her big bonnet tied with a broad bow under one ear made her look like an old-fashioned doll. Her clear, shrill voice asserted itself against the violent waves of the organ.

The Salvation Army man who accompanied her was seated on a stool, with the brass bowl for offerings on the pavement in front of him. He was trying to give his accordion the grave, swelling tones of the competing organ. The constant stream of passers-by, whether generous or indifferent, produced no change of expression on those two faces. The accordionist's was astonishingly young. His fixed, steady gaze seemed to see nothing of the people who poured past the brass bowl, now singly, now in groups. The woman sang with her eyes focused on some invisible point . . . a point above the heads of the crowd and lower than the sky. . . . Now and then, a fine, almost imperceptible rain made the asphalt glisten.

" Would you give me a few groschens? " I asked my father. He slipped two coins into my hand and I went up to the pair. ' With a swift, yet solemn gesture, as if I were voting for them, I deposited the money in the bowl.

We went into the church. The smell of incense enveloped me as if someone had flung an entangling veil over me. We found three places in the back bench and I watched, without the slightest intention of praying. In those days we were always going into churches to find a refuge, to hide ourselves, to wait or to rest. My back easily adapted itself to the hard wooden backs of the benches. But that evening, an impression struck me. The faces seemed to be fixed in their aggressive outlines. They made me think of children's drawings where the pencil lines are gone over afterwards in black ink. And, suddenly, I felt I was stifling. . . .

" When can we go? " I whispered into my mother's ear.

" We're going in a moment," she answered. " Mass is almost over."

All at once, the organ stopped. Thanks to this unexpected silence, a woman's voice penetrated into

33

the nave. It was the Salvationist's voice but her frail song shattered almost at once against the marble pillars. She stopped singing.

I was moved. And hurriedly, with modest, trembling haste, I thought of my dreams and my desires. It was not praying; it was letting my thoughts run on unbridled. In the front row, people were already getting up and I, all at sea, still had so many things to express! How I should like to write a book, several books; how I should like to begin writing this very day and go on writing all my life! And how splendid it would be to have readers too . . . and, as well as all that, a great love.

My mother and father stood up and we left the church. But, as we were walking away from it, an idea struck me. I do not remember what excuse I made, but I returned to the church. It was already dark and empty. I wanted to feel God's presence and I almost whispered in His ear: " I should also tremendously like to have a child. . . . My God, give me readers and give me children. . . ."

When I caught up with my parents, the rain was already falling heavily.

We looked for a cheap little restaurant. We found it on our way back to the Kleeblattgasse. It was marvellous, that little restaurant! A smiling waitress showed us to a tiny table covered with a paper cloth with a lacy border. Several people were dining and, from a nearby table, a smiling, made-up lady gave us an amiable nod.

34

" What does she want ? " asked Papa uneasily. " Is she a spy ? "

I did not dare glance in her direction.

The waitress approached, removed the pencil from behind her ear, and prepared to take down our order. Then, as Papa looked at the handwritten menu, he turned white.

" We haven't these food tickets they insist on. . . ."

We bent over the menu in despair.

The waitress understood at once.

" If you can pay a supplement, you can have dinner all the same."

" Right," said my father, " but bring us something to eat quickly. . . ."

When the waitress had gone, he said:

" They gave me a little money at the Reception Centre. We can just get along for two weeks, but after that . . ."

The waitress returned at last and we ate with a ferocious appetite.

The lentil soup was boiling hot. Ever since we had left Hungary, lentils pursued us! Afterwards, we each had a couple of thin, greyish Vienna sausages and a boiled potato.

I noticed an old gentleman near us who was eating with slow solemnity. He cut his little sausage into tiny, transparent slices and put a little mustard on each.

Just before we left Vienna, a kindly fellow who was showing us the way and who had realised we were

35

refugees, had cursed the war all the time he was conducting us along with exquisite politeness.

" My sister died of starvation," he told us. " Now we have everything, but, before, it was famine . . . It's along here, sir . . . this way, lady . . . the street you're looking for. . . ."

But that night, the dinner was incomparably rich.

I was entitled to have a cake; a tart that was a speciality of the restaurant. The jam was made of tomatoes and it was sweetened with saccharine instead of sugar. All the same, it was very good.

" You know," Mamma told me. " If you ask God for something the first time you go into a particular church, your prayers will certainly be answered."

" I know," I replied, radiant. " I do know, and I asked. . . ."

" Well . . . may one know your secret? "

I revealed the one that was easiest to admit.

" I prayed to have a child."

They were genuinely astonished.

A little later, when we were back in the street where our room was, Papa said to me:

" You ought to have asked for a passport for him too."

" For whom? "

" For the child. . . ."

I laughed. It was a happy evening.

I rang the bell. A man we had not seen before opened the door. We went up to the peaceful little room and, a few minutes later, we were all sleeping in real beds, wearing nightclothes and feeling free people at last.

In the morning, I was awakened by a thought. My parents were still asleep but I felt extremely clear-headed. They were delivered over to me in their unconsciousness; their faces, abandoned to heavy sleep, distressed me. The rhythm of their breathing, the total silence of that house, the stillness of our three bodies filled me with a violent despair. That day was my twentieth birthday. I had not mentioned the fact the day before, not even during dinner. I almost wanted them to forget this date; I was already prepared for a bitter disappointment. Events had gone too fast for me; I wanted to stop and recover my breath.

Perhaps, downstairs, a letter had arrived for me. A letter with a lot of stamps and several postmarks; a letter that had come from a long way off. From what country? I had no idea. A letter that had been written while we were crossing the frontier. A love-letter, a letter of waiting and hoping; a letter full of promises. I imagined an impatient, eager man, somewhere in this great world. A man who had been waiting for me for years, who had been following from afar all my adolescent joys and sorrows, a man building his life on my life. The image of the man and the image of the child became strangely intermingled. Sometimes, in my wild dreams, I was leaning over a cradle in which lay a child with a grown-up's face; a face I had composed out of a thousand details.

Saturated with analytical novels, I had often fled from an imaginary house, repeating to myself the arguments of Ibsen's Nora. And, while we were still at Fonyod, when I used to go and swim in Lake Balaton, I would often be Flaubert's gentle Emma waiting for her lover as I walked through the steep wood that led down to the shore. I invented daring dialogues. I repulsed the treacherous advances of invisible gallants who pursued me and, at the end, I flung myself into the lake as one flings oneself into a great adventure.

But the reality was very different. Before we left Fonyod, I had wanted to go to a dance organised by the young people of the village. Alas, all my pre-war clothes appeared to have shrunk. The fact was, it was I who had grown. The flowered chintz curtain which adorned our rustic dining-room was converted into a dress for me. It was the first one that did not constrict my chest. My mother gave me her only pair of high-heeled shoes.

I knew already that our exile by the lake was drawing to its close. The project of our departure, long ago conceived, cherished and ripened, was our daily topic of conversation. Nevertheless, I wanted to dance just once more in Hungary. I also wanted to be nicely bronzed for the evening and I spent the entire day on the lake shore, basking like a lizard in the warm, fine sand. But a violent sunstroke gave me a high temperature and I had to spend that much-looked-forward-to evening in bed. The days that followed were thoroughly wretched. The only diversion that remained to me was to retire completely into my dreams. I no longer went to Budapest; now that I had finished my studies, what reason was there for me to go? The doors of the future had been hermetically sealed again; even my parents' old friends looked on me as a ghost from the past. It was no longer possible to say or to hear a personal, human word. The sense of my utter uselessness in other people's lives left me absolutely crippled and helpless.

Between my own experiences concerning life, love and death there were certainly amazing discrepancies. By now I had acquired the habit of dreading every moment. I dreaded people's faces; I dreaded lips that might utter cruel words. I dreaded the darkness that brought nightmares. I had seen decomposition at work. For ten days, in front of our house in Budapest, I had watched the faces of corpses gradually becoming covered with scales like the backs of fishes. I had seen the despairing expression and the weeping eyes of the horses in Budapest, dying, inch by inch, of thirst as the days went by. I had also lived through the crazy, meaningless hours of the great bombardments when the concrete shuddered and the walls collapsed. I had seen a baby sucking at the empty, dried-up breasts of its mother. All this was mingled together in my mind. And if someone had asked me the question: " Who is the woman you would wish to be like? " I should have answered, without hesitation, " Madame Bovary! " But when a boy kissed me for the first time, I had nearly fainted; the sensation of a stranger's lips on my own had utterly overwhelmed me. . . .

And now, here I was in Vienna. I was twenty years old and everyone around me was asleep!

I got out of bed and dressed. I went down to the kitchen where Madame Wagner was already bustling about by her gas-stove. It had been agreed that she should give us breakfast.

"Good morning, madame," I said, sitting down on a chair.

"Good morning, mademoiselle," she replied amiably, but without a smile. "Would you like your coffee?"

"Yes, please."

No sooner had I sat down to it, than I realised I was hungry. From time to time, the door opened. At first, it was a man of about fifty who spoke Polish with Madame Wagner. He glanced at me furtively and with some distrust. Madame Wagner must have told him I was Hungarian and did not know a word of Polish for he seemed appeased and went on talking volubly without bothering about me. I then concentrated on eating as slowly as possible so as to see as much as I could of the life of this strange house.

There was also a taciturn young man whose nationality I could not guess as he did not utter a word.

Definitely the most interesting was a young woman

with flaming red hair, blue eyes shaded with long lashes and a magnificent body, heavy yet graceful, like a Roman statue.

After having sized me up, she smiled at me. But it was not a friendly smile; it was the smile of a woman who wants to display her teeth to another woman. I was enchanted to be the other woman.

" Just passing through Vienna? " she threw out casually though the question was pointless.

" We don't know yet whether we're staying permanently or whether we are going on somewhere else," I answered, my heart beating.

" You speak German very well," she went on, as she drank her black, unsweetened coffee.

" I learnt it at school. . . ."

At that moment, my parents arrived, tense and anxious.

" How *could* you leave the room like that without warning us? " scolded my father.

" I haven't stirred out of the house," I answered, more sharply than I meant to.

Meanwhile Madame Wagner had introduced the young red-haired woman to my mother, who looked slightly mistrustful.

" You see, madame, little Wanda is the daughter of one of my Czech cousins. She is a Czech too, and a refugee like yourselves. The poor girl lost her husband during the war. She is engaged to a charming American who is a great consolation to her and who is going to take her to New York. . . ."

41

"Delighted . . ." said Mamma, remaining strictly within the bounds of conventional politeness.

Wanda presided over my parents' breakfast. She put her elbows on the table and never once removed her advertising smile.

"I'll be back in a moment," I whispered to my father. I ran down the stairs. I wanted at least just to look in the letter-box. But, in this old door, there was no slit for letters. And suddenly I thought that, here, everyone was in transit like ourselves. No one had any papers nor any real address.

I went up to the kitchen again and, at last, for the first time, I saw some trace of real life. On the first floor, a child was looking out from a door that stood ajar next to the kitchen and watching the staircase.

"What language do you speak?" I asked in German.

By way of answer, he shut the door.

Well, that was that. . . . I went up to our room, pausing for a moment on the second floor where there were three doors. I overheard scraps of conversation in Polish. Then I retired into our own room. I looked out through the window; the street was quiet, as usual. A solitary, idle dog was sniffing into corners; he was hesitating, unable to make up his mind. . . .

Later on, when we went out, my parents told me that Madame Wagner had invited us to have tea with her. She had promised to tell them where they could get papers to leave Vienna and cross the frontier at Linz. We were in the American zone of Vienna but the city itself was surrounded by the Russian zone of Austria; the whole country, in fact, was divided up in the same way as its capital. Our aim was to get to the real West and therefore to leave the Russian-occupied territories. Madame Wagner had told Mamma that a night-train, leaving Vienna in the evening, stopped, round about midnight, at Linz. There, the Russians rigorously scrutinised the passengers' papers. Those who had Austrian identity cards could proceed on their way unmolested, but with the papers handed out to refugees, it was impossible to get through. There were thus only two solutions. Either once again to have a guide who would take us on foot and then in a boat, or to procure ourselves forged Austrian papers. Both solutions required money—the money we did not possess.

We had lunch in the same little restaurant. The friendly waitress gave us extra rations of potatoes and sausage.

" Will you still be here the day after to-morrow ? " she inquired.

" Yes, alas," my father replied mechanically. " Where else could we be ? "

" You're brave, considering your situation," said the waitress admiringly. " Very brave. . . ."

" It was more difficult crossing the frontier than it is living here," explained my mother.

The waitress nodded.

" All the same, you're very brave. . . ."

Papa lost patience.

" All right, then, we *are* brave. But why keep on saying so ? "

" Because, from the day after to-morrow, we shall be in the Russian zone," declared the girl. " For a month."

Papa dropped his cigar.

" They change the zones ? "

" Every six months."

At such a moment, I felt myself completely detached from what was going on. I felt like a builder standing on the outer scaffolding of a house and amusing himself by watching the inmates through the window. I saw my parents turn pale and the waitress's face became so definite, so clear in all its details that I can still see her long nose, her thin, nervous mouth and her frizzy hair, dull and dry from cheap permanent waves.

" Yes, indeed, my good sir," she repeated. " That's the way it is."

We swallowed our lunch very quickly and returned to the house.

Madame Wagner, in her warm kitchen, huddled against her stove, was not surprised to see us. She was knitting and her needles devoured the grey wool at disconcerting speed.

Papa asked her to return us the money we had given her for the two weeks in advance.

She shook her head.

44

"Impossible," she muttered. "Impossible."

And we could see from her face that this refusal distressed her even more than it distressed us.

"But we have absolutely no resources," my father explained gently, emphasising the words as if he were speaking to a backward child.

"And I have no resources either. A poor widow who fends for herself as best she can. . . . All my tenants are leaving to-morrow night. For me, that is a catastrophe. . . ."

Half an hour later, it as my father who was comforting *her*.

"But, Madame Wagner, why didn't you tell us yesterday about this change? You must have foreseen it."

She was snivelling, but her eyes were dry.

"How can you expect me to foresee History? And I don't like getting mixed up in high politics. In any case, I *should* have warned you, to-morrow afternoon."

Finally, my father demanded:

"But where are we going to live?"

There was a malicious little gleam in her eyes as she replied:

"At the Station Hostel. . . ."

"You are too kind, Madame Wagner," my father answered dryly.

She continued to knit without flinching. Then she added, suddenly timid and helpless:

"You could go into the French zone. It's quite

45

close, near the Graben.   Go to the French, they'll
help you. . . ."

Half an hour later, my father had left the house.
And mother and I stayed on in the warm kitchen,
silent and motionless, like objects forgotten in a corner.
Mamma was reading the *Wienerzeitung*, turning over
the pages with a sharp flick.   Each time she did so,
the sound of the paper made Madame Wagner start.
She found our hostility hard to bear; she kept giving
little sighs and letting her work slip off her lap.   Finally she got up and began to get the tea.   Out of the
corner of my eye, I noticed the number of cups on the
table.   When my mother saw these preparations, she
stood up.

" We'll go upstairs and wait for your father there."

Madame Wagner flung herself in front of the
kitchen door.

" You can't do that to me!   Refuse the tea I'm
getting ready for you. . . .   We mustn't part in anger.
In this life, you never know when we may need each
other. . . ."

In our hearts, we were frightened of her.   We were
completely at her mercy for, if Papa could obtain no
help from the French authorities, it was she who
would have to get us out of our troubles!

We stayed.   Later, Wanda arrived, accompanied
by a thin little American who was eclipsed by his
uniform as if it were a costume for a fancy-dress ball.
We shook hands and Wanda made him sit beside her
and filled his tea-cup for him.

46

The economical Madame Wagner did not switch on the electric light and we remained physically and morally stupefied in the soft dusk. The shadows gradually grew deeper and deeper, as if our own gloomy words and thoughts were increasing them. Wanda was impressive; her eyes shone and she lavished every possible attention on the American, who muttered incomprehensible words in the depths of his throat. Wanda presided over this strange tea-party. I admired her. She was the first *femme fatale* I had seen; she must have had a very murky past. She talked to Madame Wagner; her red hair, with its metallic sheen, framed a face that, expressive as it was, never gave a real smile. Afterwards, the American told a long story of which I did not understand a single word. At the beginning of it, I paid attention: I wanted to be the well-educated girl who had not spent eight years learning English for nothing. Unfortunately, I had to realise that my studies had been completely useless. He spoke in a way so different from my teacher that it amounted to another language.

The tea that Madame poured us out from time to time was becoming extremely strong. I was aware of that stale taste of tea-leaves that have been soaking for a long time in hot water; that musky taste that curdles one's saliva, coats one's palate, puts one teeth on edge and accelerates one's heartbeats. But I went on drinking all the same, like someone drinking innumerable toasts to their own projects. I knew that I should write a novel about Wanda, about her mysterious, shoddy life. I could feel episodes and details springing up in my mind; I had already decided that she should have a golden-haired friend of her own type; the type of adventuress who is resolved to retire, as soon as she is thirty, into a corner of what is called " decent " society.

She was the adventuress who wears her own body like armour and who " settles down " as soon as she sees the first dints in it; the crow's feet, the slackening chin, the breasts growing less voluptuous as they grow heavier. At that point she finds the eternal, simple-minded soldier who is capable of confusing love with the body and taking patience for tenderness. This little American here who was carrying off his European wife to one of the great cities of his own country, as one carries off a piece of loot, would never know that it was she who had made the good haul. I was already thinking about the fate of their children and trying in my mind to describe their faces. I could have warmed up the cold tea by holding the cup between my burning palms. I had divined the source of my own secret; I was at once feverish and rapturous. It was then, in the gathering dusk of that crucial afternoon, that I first drew my invisible line, my magic circle. I divided all the human beings I had known up till then into two camps; those whom I would keep as vague, floating memories and those who would take shape again, re-created or modelled by myself, on blank paper. I had completely lost all sense of reality. I was ensconced in the middle of a chapter I should one day write ... wanting to get away from this atmosphere of charming ghosts, I rose from my chair and said to my mother:

" I'm going up to my room."

" I'll join you in a few minutes," she replied.

Hurriedly, I said good-bye. Wanda's hand was warm and flabby; it was already the hand of the little bourgeoise she would soon be. The American also produced some presumably friendly words out of his throat. At last I was outside the door. I ran up the dark staircase and plunged into our room. I switched on the light and, as I passed the glass that hung over the wash-basin, I looked at myself. I was transformed. I studied myself for a long time, and suddenly, my own face became a stranger's; I had to sustain the gaze of someone who looked astonishingly like me. When I left my double, I looked feverishly for my winter coat. It was in the cupboard, on a hanger. I took it out and flung it on the bed. I had no scissors, so I tore open the stitches of the hem with my nails. Before we left Hungary, I had slipped two school exercise books into the lining. It was the diary I had kept during the siege of Budapest and which I had so often meant to burn at Fonyod. But, though I was frightened of keeping a text that might be dangerous, I had never mustered up sufficient resolution to destroy it. And now, my exercise-books were here in Vienna, at liberty! I stroked the blue paper covers which still displayed their white labels bearing my name. Once, a very short time before his death, Pista had

49

taken one of my note-books . . . I don't remember
which one . . . and said: " You're always writing,
mademoiselle. You mustn't ruin your pretty eyes."
It was the first real compliment I had received in
my life.

When my mother came in, I slipped the exercise-
books under my pillow.

" My poor child, I haven't kissed you to-day, and
to-day's your birthday! "

" It doesn't matter a bit," I replied, feeling full of
generosity. I had quite forgotten my bitter resentment of the morning. " It doesn't matter a bit. . . ."

She was close to me, sitting on the bed; weighed
down with care, anxiously listening for my father's
footsteps. She looked small, fragile and immensely
tired. My secret was on the tip of my tongue.

Before I had time to regret it, I announced:

" I'm going to write a novel, Mamma. For me,
Wanda is Vienna. I've already got at least fifteen
characters. Just imagine, how marvellous to write
the life of a woman who changes her lovers with the
zones! What do you think of the idea? "

" Appalling . . . Terrible . . . Disgusting. . . ."

She was on the defensive now and thanks to that
shred of experience I had gained in the kitchen,
I wanted to shock my mother.

" There are things one mustn't say and one mustn't
write," she added, firm and decisive.

But I was gay and sure of myself. I improvised, so
as to shatter her still more.

" I shall have a black man in this book too. He'll kill, like a sort of modern Othello."

My mother had all her hackles up when my father arrived. He brought very good news. The Refugee Aid department of the French zone had accepted us. They were going to lodge us in one of the hotels placed at their disposition and they would give us papers to cross the demarcation line at Linz.

" They're charming," repeated my father. " Charming."

After dinner, in a half-dream, I was already imagining a French fiancé for Wanda.

That night, I slept dreamlessly, with the quiet conscience of one who has accomplished a task.

# 3

THE FOLLOWING MORNING, I was dreamy, absent-minded and highly irritating to my parents. We set off very early to the Mariahilferstrasse and, in a shop, we found a cheap cardboard suitcase. It was shiny but it had a spurious elegance and it was adorned with two locks of some anæmic metal. My father was submerged in his worries. We had to leave Madame Wagner's house that very afternoon to install ourselves in the Hotel Graben. I carried the suitcase and thought of the ones we had had before the war in Budapest. They were of pigskin; their size and weight and their solid brass fittings made them a curse to porters. Those suitcases were little portable wardrobes, worthy of our slow, stately journeys. I shall never forget those journeys, or myself, a shy, spoilt child in a first-class carriage with my nose against the window and the metallic taste of tunnels in my mouth. My imagination would play round the small, silent houses the train overtook, spitting out simultaneously smoke, soot and the throbbing fury of its engine. How pretty they were, the Hungarian stations! They awaited us in the hollows of valleys, on the shore of the lake, in the heart of the cornfields, among sheaves

stacked in the shape of a cross. If I had got off the
train blindfold, I should have known each place just
by its smell. The smell of pines and streams announced the mountains; the damp mists that tasted
like tears, meant Kolozsvar. The smell of shells and
wet seaweed, that little wind carrying drops of spray,
that was the lake. In yet another place, the station
was surrounded by ripe cornfields and sweet with the
scent of acacia honey.

" What a sleepwalker! " cried Mamma because, in
crossing a road, I had looked neither to left nor right.
" Wake up, child! "

" Heedless youth," sighed my father, shrugging his
shoulders.

I shut myself up in my silence, without looking at
the swarming streets. They were full of people,
terrified of the Russians, who were hurriedly moving
house and seeking refuge in what, for the next few
months, would be the western zone.

We crossed the Burg: already the Russian soldiers
were appearing in the park full of naked trees.

" And you're dreaming," my father went on. " You
forget that we are in Vienna, with a few schillings in
our pockets, faced with an uncertain future. . . ."

No, I was far from forgetting that we were in
Vienna. I was thinking about Wanda and about my
decision of last night to write a book about her. But
I had a great problem. How could I depict an amorous
life with no experience except that one kiss whose
disturbing memory was still with me? However, to

54

reassure myself, I thought of Emily Brontë. She had been able to write *Wuthering Heights*, shut away in a vicarage, out of her virgin violence and hatred.

We arrived back in the Kleeblattgasse. Madame Wagner could not be found. My father knocked at her door for several minutes without obtaining any answer. Soon afterwards, we left the house, with the suitcase loaded with our clothes.

The Graben Hotel was in a quiet, elegant street near the Herrengasse. The great vestibule smelt of dust. The reception desk, with its empty pigeon-holes and bunches of motionless keys, was as sad as the blank gaze of a victim of amnesia vainly trying to recall his memories. The porter lowered his newspaper and watched our approach; then he took the permit my father held out to him. While he was reading it, I noticed that his hand shook slightly. At the bidding of an unseen hand, the lift set itself in motion with a mechanical sigh and slowly vanished in its cage.

" What is your nationality? " inquired the porter.

" Hungarian," my father answered, mistrustful.

Behind the rimless spectacles, the moist eyes softened.

" I was in Budapest in 1912," said the man.

He got up and spent a long time searching for a key. Key in hand, he returned from the reception-desk and signed to us to follow him. He was small and bent and he questioned us with tenacious obstinacy.

" So the French have sent you here. . . .  Will you be staying long? "

Papa did not answer.

On the third floor, he turned to the right and we followed him in silence.  The great faded red carpet muffled the sound of our footsteps.  The porter's gesture, as he opened the door of Room 43 was that of a servant, but his voice was full of contempt as he said:

" If you're not warm, tell the French to give *us* some coal too—and not only the hotel guests! "

He walked over towards the window, pulled the curtain and opened a door.

" You've got a bathroom as well.  This was a fine room before the war.  An expensive room. . . ."

My father, suddenly irritated, dismissed him.

" All right, my good man, we'll find everything we need. . . ."

The porter had gone.  So I took the key that was still hanging outside in the lock.  That key had promoted us to occupants! . . .

Mamma arranged our possessions in enormous wardrobes that contained at least fifty hangers and fifteen drawers.

I shut myself up in the bathroom with a piece of soap.  By a miracle, the water was very hot.  I stood, naked, on the little mat that bore the name of the hotel, waiting for the bath to fill and, after a few minutes, I immersed myself up to the neck in the water.  It was an extraordinary sensation; an almost painful delight. With my eyes shut and my hair drenched, I lay in the bath, covered with this wet, caressing warmth. I had the feeling that this bath was going to deliver me from all physical misery. For over a week, I had been soaked in sweat, which had sometimes run down my face mingled with tears. Now my feet, tired from long walks, stretched themselves out joyously. I could hear the nervous beating of my heart, like a far-off disquieting tom-tom.

When I came out of my bath, Mamma wanted me to lie down for a little. My father had gone out. I huddled up under the eiderdown, meaning to get up as soon as my mother had had her bath.

I did not wake up till seven o'clock in the evening. Papa was writing, bending over the table in the pink glow of the bedside lamp. His tired, absorbed face softened my heart.

" Papa . . ."

He turned towards me, smiling.

" You've slept well, my child. . . ."

" Where's Mamma? "

" She's downstairs, in the hotel kitchen. She can make us tea or coffee for after dinner. They've given her permission."

I shall always remember my stay at the Graben Hotel. What a strange, indefinite life we led there! Our bodies, at long last, had revolted. They had borne up well during the period of high tension but here, in this semi-repose in which we had nothing to do but to wait for our identity papers, they manifested

57

their displeasure. My mother's ankles were so swollen that she stayed in bed for four days. My father, with his livid face, was a prey to insomnia and I myself was constantly battling against terrible dreams. The physical and moral shock we had sustained revealed itself in this general loosening-up.

My father who, even during our exile on the shore of the lake, had been able to provide for the family needs by giving lessons was now entirely at the mercy of organisations. From morning to night, he filled up forms and interminable questionnaires. Our aim was to leave Vienna for good. Austria had been divided up between the four Powers. We wanted to get to Innsbruck, in the French zone. The officer who dealt with our affairs thought they would accept us in the Refugee Camp at Kufstein, fifty kilometres from Innsbruck. But we first had to get into the zone occupied by the Western Powers and, to do this, we had to cross the demarcation line of Enz. This was a little river near Linz. The railway bridge was guarded on one side by the Russians, on the other, by the Americans. To choose liberty as the principle of a normal life, to say that liberty is an elementary human right, is easy. The immense difficulty begins the moment one begins to take those words seriously.

In those days, at least, I did not yet know that any human being labelled with the name of " refugee " was destined to be a clown, that he was cast as the buffoon of a disintegrated Europe. He was the wretched stage character who talks and tells stories,

who tries to persuade people; the optimistic hawker
who believes in his merchandise and cries it to almost
deaf ears.

What remains in my mind of Vienna? The raw,
healthily intoxicating sensation of a discovery. The
discovery of my first foreign city. As a child, I had
been the prisoner of a small estate and great traditions.
My parents travelled while I remained in Hungary.
I had the baptism of the West without passport or
luggage. I could have recited whole passages of
*Undine*, which was marvellously translated into Hungarian, but the fact that everyone around me spoke a
language different from my own, enchanted me.
Vienna without her waltzes, Vienna famished for food,
was still charming Vienna to us—and our time there
was a time of hopes that did not yet contain any seeds
of bitterness.

I was able to buy a few sheets of white paper and a
pencil. And, while my parents made the rounds of
the offices and the various organisations, I stayed in
the hotel bedroom. I wanted to write the novel about
Wanda. I cherished her and cursed her; she sat
there beside me, invisible, mocking me with her
voluptuous smile, proudly confident of her beauty.
Everything of which I lacked experience—the whole
of life, in fact—I replaced by brutality. I revenged
myself on her, too. I had her nightdress torn to shreds
by a jealous Negro; she was knocked about by an
American who, of course, had Indian blood in his
veins; she was to be deserted by a Frenchman and

raped by a Czech. I made remorseless demands on her in the way of parting embraces, savage kisses and base betrayals. I jotted down notes for all these episodes but the list of my future chapters was so formidable that, before my parents returned, I tore it up and disposed of it down the lavatory.

To escape on my own was anything but easy. For my parents, a great city in the period just after a war, was the headquarters of the white slave traffic where bandits laid hidden traps for pure, innocent young girls. Oh, how they exasperated me with those old, out-of-date stories of theirs! I wanted a tête-à-tête with my own Vienna, an assignation with its romantic little squares, the memory of a moment that belonged only to the two of us. After my purchases of paper, I had three schillings left over. One afternoon, I went off without telling my parents. All on my own, I saw everything with a different eye. And, in the glass of a shop window, I saw myself . . . fair-haired, frail-looking and unsure of myself. If I had had some red on my lips, I should, I thought, have been almost pretty. . . .

I went into a little café and I ordered a Viennese coffee. It was there I smoked my first cigarette since our departure from Hungary. It was a Hungarian cigarette; it was half empty, because the tobacco had come out in my pocket. Opposite me was an old woman who was feeding her dog with the crumbs of her cake. Half an hour later, I left and returned to the hotel at a run.

" We were already beginning to get anxious. . . ."

I suddenly lost my temper. . . .

" Oh, Lord, do let me alone with your eternal fussing. . . ."

I have always regretted since that I was so impatient with my parents, but it is so difficult being twenty.

The next day, we went off to have ourselves photographed. It was the first automatic apparatus I had seen. A smiling Fraülein made me sit down in a tiny, violently-lit cage. She took my head in her hands and turned me towards a slanting mirror situated at the end of this species of box.

" Smile! "

I did not want to smile. I was alarmed at the idea of seeing my face fixed on shiny paper. I had spent those dead years by the lake without once having my photograph taken. I used to avoid looking-glasses; it seemed to me that, if I did not ever see myself, I should suffer less from loneliness. But here I was the prey of this glittering wild beast that wanted to burn and devour me with its blinding light! I endured six clicks and then it was my parents' turn.

Ten minutes later, they handed us the little photos in a transparent envelope. I was confronted with the velvet collar of my old winter coat and, above that collar, a drawn face in cruel relief, obstinately fair hair and black eyebrows.

My parents were executed in the same manner. Three heads of criminals; three faces of morons; three grotesque profiles. It was the new technique.

Two days later, we received three forged Austrian identity cards. I saw my photo again; it bore the name of Elise Meyer. Neither the face nor the name belonged to me. Were we free or had we lost our memories?

I was the daughter of this Meyer family. At all costs, we must avoid uttering a word in the train. We were Austrians, going to stay with friends of theirs in Innsbruck. "Don't give yourselves away by your accent. The Russians are strict; it's their last chance of controlling people's movements. They're hard; they look suspiciously at all the passengers and their papers. Naturally, you're taking a considerable risk. If you're lucky. . . . If not, they'll hand you over to the Hungarian authorities."

Fear rendered us silent. On the evening of our departure, we crept down the stairs with a cat-like tread.

"Are you leaving?" the porter shot at us. "Haven't made a long stay, have you?"

We walked along the icy street to the tramway. We still did not say a word. Our lives were in danger. But if, the next morning, we were at Innsbruck, it would be real freedom at last!

Silently, I said good-bye to Vienna, with my eyes full of tears. I was at the beginning of those years when they filled with tears at the slightest provocation.

At eight o'clock precisely we were on the platform, jammed in the middle of quite a large crowd. There were some American Negro soldiers; near us stood a grave nun, with an enormous starched butterfly on her head and, farther away, two Russian soldiers.

The train arrived, throbbing and clanking, and we took our place in a compartment. There was room for three on the wooden seats. I sat beside my mother, near the window and the nun made up the third. Papa took the place opposite me; next to him were two civilians; a seedy man and a woman with a big basket on her knees. I was aware of an obstinate little pain in my neck. It was a vein that was throbbing hard, as if I had another heart under my left ear. The real heart was drumming against my chest with heavy, irregular thuds. I wanted to be sick. I would have liked to tell my parents that it would be better to get off the train and go back to our vegetative life at the hotel, for this tension was unendurable. I could not even ask what time it was, because, once installed in the train, I could no longer put the question either in Hungarian or in my German whose accent would betray me. I knew that the train left at half-past eight and that we should reach the crucial bridge twenty minutes before midnight. Three hours and forty minutes of travelling.

The train left the station without a jolt, as if it were sliding down a slope. That sensation of accelerated speed went right through my whole body. I closed my eyes, wanting to sleep or, at least, pretend to sleep, but it was impossible. Condemned to silence, I was brimming over with ideas. . . . I could have kept up a feverish and excited conversation all through the night. How humiliating it was to be so frightened and to be holding blindly to luck with a kind of inward imploration. And all that for a displacement of a few kilometres. One was an occupier or a liberator, according to whether one were born in the East or the West. But, between the two, there was only a shifting waste of waters that ebbed and flowed at the mercy of the political tide. As I sat there, with my eyes open and my face against the window fogged by my breath, I felt nothing but hatred for the train. Outside, the universe was black. I could not discern a single light. To think that, if the Russians discovered us, it meant returning to Hungary! When we had crossed the frontier on foot, and were too exhausted to go on, we had at least been able to lie down on the wet earth and hide our faces in a heap of dead leaves. But this train was rushing along at a crazy speed like a travelling morgue with its corpses sitting on wooden benches. I looked down mechanically at my feet. If only I could slip under the seat and hide myself!

Mamma was dozing or, rather, pretending to doze. There was a nervous tic in her left eyelid; the spasm had a rhythm of its own and made her whole face quiver. My father was staring at some invisible point; I was in his field of vision but he was looking right through me. If only the real Austrians with us did not notice our terror! . . . What could this respectable Meyer family be frightened of? The thin man beside my father had finished reading his paper; he folded it up and, absent-mindedly, let it slip to the floor. I did not dare either to pick it up or to ask if I could look at it, though the time would have passed more quickly with that paper. The door of the compartment opened with a creak and an Austrian inspector walked through, leaving the opposite door open too. Wasn't that a sign that we should soon be there? Mamma opened her eyes, but her left eyelid went on rebelliously twitching. The man picked up his paper, and the nun clutched the crucifix of her big, heavy rosary between her fingers. The man opposite began chatting with the woman beside him, who was peeling an apple over her basket. Mamma looked at me; she was hungry too. The woman shared the apple with the man, who ate it greedily. They were all talking now and this buzz of voices seemed to emphasise our muteness.

Outside, there suddenly appeared lights. The train slowed down; then stopped. Words of command, yelled out by the Russians, rent the night. Once again, those voices, *their* voices. They made us shudder in a European train; they made us feel alone in the midst of a crowd and turned a journey into a nightmare. My father slipped his hand inside his jacket, no doubt meaning to take his identity card out of his pocket; he did not see my mother's disapproving glance and she had to say, in German:

" Wait . . . not yet . . . Wait till they ask for it. . . ."

The man opposite stared at us as if he had noticed our presence for the first time and the nun looked at her rosary.

65

The critical, agonising moment arrived. The Russians came into our carriage. The one who was examining the identity cards wore a fur cap; his eyes ran indifferently over the passengers, comparing faces with photographs. When he came to our row, he glanced at mine, then down at the identity card. He found the likeness perfect. Afterwards, he took my mother's papers, then my father's. Everything was in order. The man beside my father was holding another apple in his left hand. Suddenly, I realised that he was eating because he was frightened. The Russian took his card, looked at it and said a few rapid words to the other Russian. The man, frozen like a statue with half his apple in his hand, waited, as if hypnotised. The buzz in the compartment had stopped; everyone was silent, everyone was listening but no one dared turn their head or even look. The Russian made a sign to the man and said to him, in German:

" Get out. . . ."

The man stood up, his face livid. His eye-sockets were dark, like septic wounds; his gaze fastened on us avidly; he trembled like an animal caught in a trap. I thought he was going to jump out of the window, even right through the glass pane, if that was the river out there in the darkness.

" *Davaj*," said the Russian, and, pulling down the window, he yelled something to the others outside, standing by the train. It was the scream of the bird of prey, swooping down on its victim.

The man left the train, accompanied by a soldier, and the inspection went on. We remained in our places, utterly spent, like puppets whose invisible manipulating strings have been cut. The nun was praying; her thin lips were shaping words. For whom was she praying? For the unknown man?

This eternity of waiting plunged me into a state of trance I had never experienced before. The sweat ran down my back and my face was damp all over. I did not want to go on seeing my parents' ravaged faces. I shut my eyes so that I could abandon myself completely to my dreams. I would have liked to go to a country where there were no more controls. In any case, I wanted to leave Europe. At Kufstein, we should have the possibility of choosing a country as one chooses a fabric in a shop. Perhaps the solid island upheld by the pillars of a great tradition, England. . . . Or far from Europe; Australia or South America.

The train started off again, slowly and jerkily, like an invalid making his first tentative steps. We were on the bridge; the flickering lights of Linz were drawing nearer. It was evident that we really were saved.

The train stopped again. The nun turned her head towards me. I risked a faint, shy smile. She smiled back at me.

The door of the compartment opened and the three representatives of the three Powers entered. The French officer saluted everyone, just brushing his finger against his cap. The English one held out his hand for our papers and the huge American unscrewed a large oblong tin. Without warning us, he sprinkled us as if we were herrings to be salted. He pulled my father's coat open and threw a little more of this yellow dust inside it. Papa was so much surprised by this that he did not even make an instinctive gesture of annoyance. The nun's shoulders turned yellow too. Mamma received most of the powder on her back and the rest on the bodice of her dress. The American could shake the D.D.T. without risk to himself for he was wearing gloves. He undid the top button of my winter coat and I received the cold, stinging powder on my neck. I must have given a sudden jerk, for my cheek too was covered with D.D.T. It was the last straw and my resistance completely gave way. I buried my head on Mamma's shoulder and burst into tears.

Later, when the train was safely running through the American zone, we ventured out into the corridor so as to be able to talk, but, since the disinfecting process, we had nothing left to say to each other. We were on the soil of a free Europe; the train had become friendly, almost a trusted ally. I opened the window; the cold air was like a bath in pleasant, refreshing reality. Back in the compartment, I huddled into my corner and, utterly tired and worn-out, I tried to sleep. A passenger switched off the main light and we sat motionless, like embalmed corpses, faintly lit by a mysterious blue glimmer, like the night-light in a hospital ward.   After all, what were we but hospital cases on the long sick-list of History?

A young couple, who had got into the train at Linz, were already asleep.   For both of them, it was an ordinary, uneventful journey; they had not had to cross the Styx to find happiness again.   The pregnant wife held her large, soft hands over her stomach to protect the sleep of the unknown human being who was going to be born.   How miserable that journey was for *me*, with my clothes sticking to my uneasy body, with those blue shadows on my face that had never known any real girlhood and the dull aching of a mind that was already inclined to melancholy! . . . In the dimness, my father's features composed a strange mask in which old age mingled with startled surprise.   My mother, in her sleep, was clinging pathetically to her dream, as if she realised she must not move in case she woke up.   So as not to crush her starched cornette, the nun kept very upright as she dozed, but every now and then she felt herself swaying forward.   This gave her a kind of fright, but she promptly recovered her balance.

Outside, the night betrayed none of its secrets. Outside there was liberty, but it was vague and featureless.   What were we seeking here?   Where had we come from and whither were we going?   In my half-sleep, I was all incertitude.   I should have liked to be twenty years older, to have formed definite opinions and habits.   I should have liked to call up my memories but there was nothing in me but an

69

immense avidity. I was at once rebellious and thankful; I reached out towards everything, ready to taste and savour and touch. I wanted to chase away the shadows and replace them by sharp, physical impressions.

And then, miraculously, outside it began to be day. At first it was only a little grey rift, infinitely far away. Then the train was galloping in the heart of a rosy mist; the dawning colours seemed to be pasted against the damp pane; the blue lamp lost its malevolent power and the sleeping faces became marvellously young; free of wrinkles and free of thoughts. It was as if angelic, brainless children were travelling in a blue and silver tunnel. The nun leant back, relaxed, against the hard wooden seat; she was dreaming; her pearly, transparent skin had a soft blue shimmer on it like reflections from a sapphire. Everything gleamed and shone; it was the festival of the dawn.

The young husband, opposite me, stretched and yawned. But the miracle had been accomplished. It did not matter that the magic had gone out of the atmosphere; I knew, I had seen with my own eyes that there were daybreaks like that. . . . And so, from that day on, I have loved the dawn. . . .

# 4

THE REAL MORNING, grey, cold and hostile, overtook us in the midst of immense mountains. The horizon had shrunk till it was no wider than the railway track. The Inn, green, capricious and turbulent, with its fierce torrents and its waves edged with white foam, followed the train, which was going at full speed. Sometimes, on the top of a proud peak, the ruins of a fortified castle would appear. The atmosphere of the compartment was thick and poisonous with stale breath. The future mother, heavy in her pregnancy, was visibly hungry; she was nibbling a biscuit and trying not to lose a crumb of it. All the faces were swollen from a bad night's sleep; I looked at my hands; they were dirty. My fingers were hurting me; it was a grumbling pain, discreet but obstinate. I owed it to the damp cellar where I had lived during the siege of Budapest; the water ran down the walls stained with saltpetre. I had never felt the cold, impressive contact of a valuable ring, but that pain that I carried in my joints, that went with me everywhere and that woke me up took the place of the ring.

At last, we arrived at Innsbruck. Mamma stepped down from the train as nervously as a shipwrecked passenger having to climb down a rope-ladder to reach the lifeboat. As we left the station, which stood in the centre of the town, I felt crushed by those assertive overpowering mountains that encircle Innsbruck. In Hungary, you have to travel for a whole day to catch sight, far away, of the bluish chain of mountains; you have time to get used to them. But here they were right on top of us, as cold and indifferent in their whiteness as enormous sugar-loaves.

It was very cold. The sun shone on the snow-covered peaks. The streets were bustling and full of tourists. A band of youths passed by us; they were carrying skis on their shoulders. A girl looked at us with interest; her red pullover was as vivid as a scarlet poppy. In my winter coat, which was black, I felt like a crow in all this immaculate whiteness. But soon the snow melted under our feet. After that, we floundered in puddles of greyish water. Near the station, we hastily swallowed a cup of coffee; we had to get as soon as possible to the office that registered and placed the refugees. We had to reach the camp at Kufstein that very afternoon.

Then began a perfect orgy of questioning and inter-rogations. We filled up forms till we had cramp in our fingers. The offices were well heated; the em-ployees all had the same monotonous voice; it was a soporific atmosphere after a sleepless night. How difficult it was to reconstruct how one had spent one's time during the last ten years! . . . Where were you in 1938? . . . At school . . . I was nine and a half at that time . . . Of which party were you a member?

... I was a Girl Guide ... What have been your
principal changes of abode since that year? ... The
space for the answers was very limited; one had to
invent another, more concentrated language in order
to satisfy the authorities. I could say yes; I could say
no; I could cross out something that did not apply.
But there was no room for any of the finer shades!
These questionnaires demanded an answer in morse
code; a biography in telegraphese.

About four o'clock in the afternoon, the official
gave us new identity cards. He put a pad in front of
us and indicated the empty square under the photos.

" Your fingerprints, please. . . ."

Feeling suddenly very hot, I brushed my thumb
lightly over the pad. The official saw that we were
novices at the job of being refugees. He helped me
by taking my thumb in his cold hand and forced me
to rub it hard on the greasy pad. While my parents
in their turn were performing the same operations,
I studied the design of my thumb. There were wavy,
parallel lines that formed concentric rings in the
middle. Did the fingerprint of a criminal differ
greatly from mine? This paper also bore witness to the
fact that we had been disinfected. As we left the office,
I had a fit of giddiness and Mamma had to sit down
on the bench in the corridor. We had had nothing to
eat since this morning and it was now half-past four.
In three-quarters of an hour, our train left for
Kufstein. How often we had heard of that little town
at school! This was because the Hapsburgs had im-

prisoned a great many Hungarian patriots in its castle.

Soon we found ourselves back in the street leading to the station. Only a little while ago, the weather had been marvellous; weather for winter sports and scarlet pullovers, just as the prospectuses announced. But now dirty, ragged clouds covered the sky and a spiteful wind flung hail full in our faces. It was refugees' weather. . . .

An ill-heated little train took us to Kufstein, where we arrived at half-past seven, in a snow-storm. Outside the station, a railwayman showed us the way to the camp and we set off through the badly-lit streets. I walked with my teeth clenched and kept blowing my nose to stop it from freezing. We did not say a word to each other. In the misty light of the street lamps, I looked out for a signpost or an arrow indicating the way to the camp.

And then the moment came when we found ourselves in front of a lowered barrier. We had reached our goal. A sentry came out of his box, examined our papers in the light of his pocket-torch and said something to us in Russian. It produced a very disagreeable impression. Here, too? Were we not far enough away, even now? The man pointed out a distant, lit-up hut, raised the barrier and we crossed the frontier of the camp of Kufstein. In that snow-storm we could only just make out the multitude of sombre buildings; only here and there did a window show a light. Soaked to our very bones, we entered the office of the camp where a woman official received us. We stood in front of her; she had red hair and wore spectacles with metal frames.

" You're Hungarian, all three of you, aren't you? " she said.

" Yes."

" I'll call the head of the Hungarian section at once."

She spoke German with a strong accent and, at last, she made us sit down. I could still go on living, but I no longer wanted to. I wanted to go to sleep here permanently, in this still warmth. I was no longer even hungry.

The Hungarian, who came in, shook the snow off his shoes, said " Good evening " to the woman, and held out his hand.

" You've arrived late," he said. " Have you had anything to eat? "

" No."

" I'm going to take you over to the canteen so that you can at least have some soup to-night."

We followed him. The canteen resembled the one at the Station Hostel and the woman who gave us the soup spoke Russian. . . .

" Why are there so many Russians here? " inquired my mother.

Our new friend shrugged his shoulders.

" They're Ukrainians; most of them were in Vlassov's army."

I did not know who Vlassov was and I had no desire to know.

75

After we had had some very hot soup, we went out once more into the snowstorm. The Commandant walked in front of us, with a torch in his hand. I could feel the water running inside my shoes; the soles had already been so thin in Vienna! He walked the length of a row of huts; the feeble lights were not bright enough to outline the mysterious shapes that were blotted out by the whirling snow.

" Here we are," he said, making his way into one of the huts.

We found ourselves in an immense, dark corridor, crammed with doors on either side and buzzing with various noises. Here, everything smelt of onions and urine. The man tried to open the seventh door on the right. The rebellious key went on turning round and round endlessly in the lock. It needed ten minutes' work before we could go in. What we entered then was a cold room, with three iron bedsteads, meagrely lit by a feeble bulb fixed to the ceiling. There was also a wardrobe. In the middle stood a table stained with large, oily smears, and two chairs.

" You're extremely lucky," he observed. " Your predecessors, who went away a week ago, have. left you a stove."

The stove was indeed there, huddled in a corner, like a sick animal.

Our guide made a slight gesture and said, in an uncertain voice.

" I forgot to introduce myself. My name is Karpai . . . Colonel Karpai. . . ."

My mother nodded and smiled, but, a moment later, she asked:

" Do you really think one can live here? "

My father stood there, motionless; he was still carrying the suitcase. Everything was so dirty that he still did not dare put it down.

The colonel was optimistic.

" It's always difficult when one first arrives, madame, but to-morrow, I'll help you. . . . You must set about organising your future life. . . . The shops are only open in the morning. . . ."

" The shops? " repeated my father ironically. " We have no money."

" Then so much the better," replied Karpai, " so much the better. You'll get everything you need here free. I'll say good night to you now. Don't forget that, at last, you have no more troubles . . . you're at home. . . . The water is at the end of the corridor, by the W.C."

He went away and we remained in our " home."

Mamma sat down on one of the grey mattresses; it was all covered with stains. With disgust, she fingered the blankets that were stiff with the chilled sweat of other people. My father examined the surroundings as if he were looking for some lost article. It was at that moment that we heard, for the first time, the close, almost confidential voice of an unknown woman. The woman was humming, but where was she? Mechanically, I glanced under the beds. I opened the cupboard; there was nothing but some grey blankets.

The voice followed my movements; it was humming a sentimental song: " Lili Marlene." And, now, a man was speaking:

" I've told you already you mustn't lick the knife. . . ."

We listened, paralysed. How could one lick a knife and hum at the same time?

The man became annoyed.

" If you go on sucking that knife, I'll slap you. . . ."

There was some muttering, then the woman began to sing, articulating the words very clearly.

" *Uber der kaserne, in dem grossen Tal. Steht eine Laterne.* . . ."

There came the noise of a resounding slap. A child howled and the woman went on:

" *Wie einst, Lili Marlene . . . wie einst, Lili Marlene.* . . ."

A second feminine voice intruded on the scene.

" If you smack Géza again, you just see what I'll do! "

" I *shall* smack him, because he's insufferable. And you won't do a thing. . . ."

And, once again, the indefatigable singer repeated: " *Wie einst, Lili Marlene.* . . ."

She was our neighbour on the right. The family, where a child was licking a knife, were our neighbours on the left.

" She hasn't a large repertoire," said Papa, lighting the remains of a cigar.

How far away morning seemed! Should we ever get to it?

I stood up on one of the chairs and hung a blanket up on some big rusty nails in the embrasure of the window. Under my bed, I discovered a little heap of coal and some wood, wrapped up in an old newspaper.

While mother was fussing round the beds, I lit the fire. But, two minutes later, the stove belched out whirling gusts of dense smoke. Instead of being warmed, we had to open everything so as to make a draught. We left the room a prey to the savage wind and took refuge, shivering, in the corridor. The neighbouring family's door opened and a young woman came out, carrying a chamber-pot. She stared at us and vanished in the direction of the W.C. A few minutes later, she returned.

" Are you, by any chance, Hungarian ? " she asked us, hiding the empty chamber-pot behind her back.

" Alas, we are," said my father.

I could see he was at the end of his tether.

" Wait a moment," said the woman. She went into her room and reappeared, two minutes later.

" Come into our room for a little. . . ."

We accepted her invitation joyfully. In their home, it was warm. A small, kindly man shook hands with us. A little boy, just beginning to walk, climbed up on the bed with disconcerting speed. Mechanically, I looked round for the knife.

Then our neighbours offered us their boiling-hot coffee and their open hearts with the spontaneous generosity of Hungarians. He was a shoemaker in Budapest; they had come there a year ago with the child asleep under a drug. They explained the rules of our new life to us; they promised to leave us all the things they did not need any more; they were going off, in three days, to Venezuela.

We stayed talking to them for a long time. The child fell asleep in his mother's arms. We spoke in low voices, as if we were afraid life would overhear us during these indefinite moments when we were waiting on the brink of events. Stupefied by the warmth and the unexpected peace, I looked at them all. The faces were drawn by a giant hand that, by preference, used black shadows but emphasised eyes and foreheads with patches of white light. The shoemaker was telling us about Venezuela; his wife listened devotedly; the child, pink and heavy, slept with parted lips, from which a trickle of saliva drooled.

" What a fate! . . ."

Who had said those words? Words and faces melted away into a soft, unreal blur.

" Let's go . . . you're almost asleep," said my mother.

We returned to our own icy room and lay down on the beds, wearing our winter coats and with our hats pulled down over our ears. I was shivering so much that I drew one of the dirty blankets over my head.

" Dear God, make the morning come soon . . . make the morning come soon. . . ."

# 5

OUR FIRST DAYS at Kufstein were like a nightmare. If
we did not have to make a fire by rubbing two sticks
together, it was thanks to our friends who guided us
through the labyrinth of the camp. During the war,
this sinister city of huts had belonged to the German
army and, after the war, it had become the haven of
the refugees. Kufstein, in my eyes, was an enormous
orphanage, in which the children abandoned by their
unnatural mother, Europe, could begin their life again
in the artificial incubator of an international organisation. All these elderly orphans were fed, clothed,
registered and examined in precisely the same way.
I was not at all ungrateful to Fate for, at that period,
the quality of all our personal feelings depended
entirely on a comparison that was easy to make. The
freedom of the West was, for us, a living miracle and
Hungary no longer appeared as anything but a vast
prison. But the fact that Hungary was no longer
anything but a prison and that life compelled us to
live as parasites was a tragedy. We kept saying to
each other, in the same breath: " What a joy to be
here . . ." and " We're reduced to *this* place. . . ." I
simply let myself drift aimlessly on the tide of events.

The medical examination had established that I was in good health; a little under-nourished but, then, who was not? . . . Fragile in appearance, but robust enough for work. I can still feel on my back the cold touch of the fingers that sounded me. I felt convinced that I should retain blue bruises for the rest of my life. The X-ray photograph demonstrated that I had a heart and lungs of iron. The oculist stared into my eyes with a little lighted mirror. The room was dark and he held my head with one hand and bent over my eye with the intense curiosity of someone spying on a secret through a keyhole. I could smell his breath and a blinding bead of white light wandered about inside my brain. Suddenly, I had the terrifying notion that what he was really doing was spying on my soul. A little later, when I tried to read the illuminated letters on his blackboard, I discovered that my eyes had grown weaker in the cellar; I had written too much by the light of a single candle.

All those eyes staring at the blackboard, how habituated they all were to gazing on grief! . . . The camp spent a great deal of money on glasses and Lithuanians, Ukrainians, Hungarians, Spaniards and Russians contemplated their liberty through steel-rimmed spectacles.

The countries that seemed most accessible were full of reservations about us. Australia had a great weakness for teeth. She did not like them to have stoppings in them. Australia wanted strong, vigorous beings, full of *joie-de-vivre*, with white teeth solidly planted in impeccable jaws. Australia repelled the unmarried with disgust; to be welcomed there, you had to have a wedding-ring. I got all the information I could about England. The island that was so high in my esteem and so misty in my imagination was lacking in nurses for mental hospitals. England had a definite preference for male nurses because, as I learnt, the insane are extremely strong when they are enraged, which they frequently are. There was still another possibility, to be a miner. As for emigration to America, it was conditioned by so many rules and regulations that the mere list of the main questions and the essential conditions to be complied with made up a thick little book. I had to think about learning a trade. But, in our hearts, we had no desire to emigrate. We were fated to be Europeans and my parents were glad that they had passed the age-limit for the exodus. Here, at Kufstein, there was the name of a different country on every lip. . . .

Thanks to our friend the shoemaker, we had become capitalists. He and his wife had given us an enormous number of useful things before they left. So we were able to bring back our lunch and our dinner from the canteen and eat them in our room, and, with the aid of the electric heater, we made our breakfast ourselves.

I had become incredibly sensitive and thin-skinned and my reflexes were so instantaneous that the mere contact of an object or even the mere awareness of a look was enough to make me tremble. I was tense and restless in this false security and I had not the bliss of being alone, since I was shut up in the same room with my parents. How miserable and detestable it was to have to dress and undress while the others turned their backs! And, besides, one was always being woken up during the night by noises coming from all over the place. Our neighbour on the right, the indefatigable singer, was a mad Lithuanian woman who had seen her entire family executed and who had been planted here by chance or by a pitiful Fate. She related her story to everyone. When I caught sight of her, I fled; her blue eyes that looked like a hunted animal's gave me gooseflesh. The room that had belonged to the family who had gone to Venezuela was now occupied by a young Jugoslav couple. They appeared to make love from morning till night, and from night till morning with the same rhythm and the same moanings. Those intolerably long winter days took away from me any impulse and even the very power to smile.

My parents had made the acquaintance of the Hungarian colony and, one after the other, all these people told their story: " When I crossed the frontier ... the moon ... the dogs ... Was the barbed-wire already up when you crossed? ... The guide ... But, of course, we're going ... to the Argentine, perhaps ... the country of the future ... My son is an engineer ... That is, he has still one more year to do at Innsbruck University. ...

The young man in question always appeared at

Kufstein on Saturday nights. He was tall, clumsy, already beginning to grow bald, and in sight of his diploma. He wanted to get married before he went abroad. All these youths had the same fixed idea; to select a continent and a wife. . . . What was I doing in their midst? . . . A medical student also wanted to marry me because he had picked Australia. How I loathed myself, seeing myself through their eyes! Dressed in clothes from unknown donors, I felt like a grotesque mannequin in a dress parade of charity garments.

Those garments arrived regularly in great corded, disinfected bales and they brought us friendly messages from all the peaceful corners of the earth. Once, I spent a whole afternoon helping to distribute them. I shall never forget that mountain of shoes, all new, but dating from the First World War. They were museum pieces that had aged without ever being worn, preserved alike from sunshine and from rain. There were ladies' shoes in yellow kid, trimmed with white doeskin; there were bootees; there were gaiters with little black buttons, and boots for slim ankles hidden under softly rustling skirts. When a pair of mauve satin boots appeared, the feeble electric bulb in the hut lost its yellow light and began to glitter like a chandelier and I could see an enormous golden circus ring and a blonde, voluptuous bareback rider who went through her act, dreaming of those lilac boots. The factory must have gone bankrupt before she could buy them and, twenty years later, the boots were resuming their interrupted career at the camp of Kufstein. But who would wear them?

The dresses with their waists round their hips came out of those old Charlie Chaplin films in which the heroines had heart-shaped mouths and foreheads covered with coy little curls under hats pulled down over their ears. But those dresses were not new. Under their arms, stained half-moons indiscreetly bore witness to emotions of long ago; to other people's heat and other people's sweat. All this stuff had been disinfected by the passage of time and by the foresight of the authorities. Nevertheless, I handled those clothes with the deliberate stoicism of a nurse, who uses her reason to master her disgust, in the name of science, so as to preserve her self-control. After the free shop in the camp was closed, I dressed myself up à la Mae West under the amused eyes of a fat Ukrainian woman who was in charge of the shop that week. I put on long suède shoes and tried to balance my weight on their fantastically high heels. I put on one of the outmoded vamp's dresses—the metallic smell of the disinfectant filled my nostrils—and, for want of a glass, I looked at myself in the smoked surface of the window-pane.

The woman looked at me too; her cunning eyes taking in every detail of my appearance. She had three long white hairs on her chin and her yellowish false teeth behind her bloodless lips made her look like an old she-cat waiting to pounce on the last mouse of her life. She came close to me and suddenly put her big, bony hands round my waist. I recoiled, startled, and she told me, in a few words of German, that I was pretty. I hastily put on my ordinary clothes again, and, leaving the shop in disorder, I hurried back to our room. Later on, we received some modern clothes but I wanted to keep my Budapest winter coat. It had been made by an admirable tailor for my fifteenth birthday; it was well nipped-in at the waist, there was a double row of buttons down the front and the collar and cuffs were of navy-blue velvet. More or less well equipped with these worn garments, and with a shy smile on our lips, we took part in the life of the camp. My father found a lending-library in the little town of Kufstein so, at least, we were able to read. I often went to the little chapel that had been set up in one of the huts, and, with despairing tenacity, I tried to find some relief, some feeling of peace in it. But my trouble was elsewhere and neither the wheezy harmonium nor my forced fervour allayed it completely.

Spring was coming and I had the stifling sense of not having caught up with life. Dawn was lighter and, by four o'clock, I was already awake. Restrained by my parents' breathing, I would lie motionless on my mattress with my eyes open, waiting. I was incubating an undefined love as one incubates an illness. I wanted to love someone? But whom? Whom could I love? Like a captive, I wanted to go away with the daylight to some other life. In the seeming immobility of those sorrowful days, I was preparing my own escape.

With the pocket-money the camp gave its grown-up orphans, I went off for a day in Innsbruck. I wanted to breathe freely, to be away from my parents and to see the French Consulate at close quarters.

From the age of five, I had learnt to love France as one loves a distant, brilliant, radiantly kind relative. At fourteen, Balzac had been for me the rich, solid nourishment that strengthens the adolescent mind and makes it grow; I was swallowed up in that monumental work. Afterwards, came the lightning-stroke of Stendhal; then I ventured into the unknown territory of Maupassant and came to love the pages of Giraudoux as one loves the memory of a man who died young. Mamma sometimes used to sing Lucienne Boyer's songs—*Je me sens dans tes bras, si petite, si petite auprès de toi*—and, with many tremors, I read *Les Thibault*. At ten, I saw the harsh face of Jouvet; he was the hero of a film that was certainly unsuitable for children. Nor shall I ever forget those great evenings in the theatre, when I was hidden in a corner of the box, and the marvellous moment when the curtain rose on *Madame Sans-Gêne* or on *La Dame aux Camélias*. And how I loved *Les Femmes Savantes* and *Tartuffe* too. It was all this that I wanted to find again in the French Consulate at Innsbruck.

In the little entrance hall, the lethargic receptionist made me sit down at a little table with two questionnaires to fill up. It was there that I saw Georges

88

for the first time. He was sitting very upright on a bench, wearing a high-necked pullover and there was something pathetic about his oval face and fair hair. He was looking at me with his grey eyes and holding a passport in his hand. As I began to study my questionnaires again, I was aware of his gaze.

He got up and came over to me.

" Would you like me to help you to fill up the questionnaire? "

" How did you know I was Hungarian? " I asked without looking at him.

" By your accent. . . . When you spoke to the receptionist. . . . If I can be of any use. . . ."

The door of the office opened and a woman called him in. He disappeared.

I was left alone with the two forms and I filled them in in block letters. I explained that I wanted a job in France and that I should be an ideal children's governess. After a while, Georges returned and it was my turn to be summoned into the office. I was very soon made aware that I was nursing a ridiculous hope in trying to settle in France. Had I been a miner or a farm labourer, it would have been child's play, but, according to the woman who interviewed me, France was overflowing with governesses. I had a mental vision of an army of foreign girls—Swedish, English, Irish, Dutch—marching on Paris under the special banner of nursery governesses. Without a nationality, what chance should I have in this avalanche of women? The bourgeoisie does not like stateless nurses.

" But we're in the French zone," I dared to point out. " I thought it was easier to get to Paris from the French zone."

" It's not a question of zone, mademoiselle. The principles of a country that is defending its integrity are always honourable. . . . You must realise that, if we let everyone come in . . ."

I left her with the extremely unpleasant feeling of being defeated.

Georges was waiting for me in the entrance-hall and among the draughts of chill spring wind he introduced himself with as much easy grace as if he had been in a drawing-room in Budapest. I learnt his name and his surname.

" May I walk along with you? "

" I'm going to the station; I must get back to Kufstein by the five o'clock train."

We walked towards the station in the fine rain.

" Are you going to France? " he inquired.

" I should have liked to go, but it's too complicated."

The lights of Innsbruck were coming on and the asphalt gleamed.

In a moment of absent-mindedness, I looked at Georges. He was a charming boy. He told me that he was soon going off to Peru, where his best friend, with whom he had been at school for eight years, had found a silver mine.

In the rain that had begun to fall, the enormous mountains were being blotted out by thick, grey clouds. I was once more conscious of the dampness. I had been given some Australian shoes at the camp shop, but I had put on my Budapest ones to come to the Consulate.

" It's very hot in Lima," he told me. " I shall have a horse and a riding-whip and Indian servants."

" How old are you? "

" Twenty-three. . . ."

" And what did you do in Budapest? "

" I was a law student. I was supposed to become a high-up in the Diplomatic like my father and law is essential for that career. . . . But I've left Hungary for good and I'm going to Peru. . . ."

We arrived at the station. I took out my return ticket and showed it to the collector. Georges returned with a platform ticket. I held out my hand to him:

" Good-bye, and have a good journey. . . ."

" Thank you," he said, and he remained standing there in the rain. I watched him through the train window.

That night, at Kufstein, I was very depressed. My father knew of this boy's family; he said his father was a well-known man. Before I went to sleep I thought that, if he had not been going to Peru, I might have loved him.

During the Siege, I had seen so many dead young men lying on the pavements of Budapest and had

91

such a vivid recollection of those astonished, glassy-eyed faces and those wide-open mouths, frozen in the effort of snatching one last breath, that it would have been hard for me to be insensible to Georges's living charm. The very time we were living in was his ally. His youth was not a mere detail, but a positive merit. The rolled collar of his pullover added the necessary imaginative touch and his plan of going-off to Peru lent him an aureole of unflinching courage. There was a discreet, romantic elegance about his gesture of farewell as he stood on the platform with his golden head bare in the rain.

I had told him my name before the train left, so he was able to write to me. His first letter arrived a week later, from Paris. I had a strange shock, almost a feeling of faintness when I saw his writing. The letter, insignificant in itself, assumed the importance of a message from beyond the grave. Georges's handwriting was exactly like my uncle's. How many times, on his desk in the Rue Notre Dame, I had seen similar well-balanced lines that looked almost engraved in the very black ink on the white paper. It was a handwriting full of wisdom and kindliness, whose round letters were linked by tiny, subtle curves. Those little signs, obedient bearers of calm thoughts and historical references, invariably grew smaller towards the end of a page and resumed their normal size at the beginning of the next. My uncle wrote to me frequently. I was pleased and proud when I received cards from him announcing presents and agreeable surprises.

The outmoded handwriting of this almost unknown young man spoke of Paris and his approaching departure. The result of that letter was that I took to drawing his profile, gilded by a foreign sun, everywhere and on everything. I needed neither pencil nor paper; I traced its invisible contours on the darkness of night, against the green leaves of a late spring and, when I went to the lending library, on the very road before my feet.

This unexpected letter, whose passport was the resemblance between the two handwritings, produced quite a sensational effect on my parents. " What? . . . You got into conversation with a total stranger and he has the audacity to write to you? What impertinence —and what times we live in! . . . Yes, the father is a remarkable man, but that doesn't prove the son is too! . . . All the same, there is no doubt that he is decent and honourable because his handwriting is really good, extraordinarily good. . . . An astonishing resemblance. . . ."

I listened to all this with unfeigned indifference, even with a slight contempt, and, according to my capricious moods, I now loved, now hated my parents. My frustrated, inwardly seething life, had destroyed my capacity to smile politely and say friendly nothings. I was always on the defensive and in a state of suspended animation; I knew that the mere fact of having survived a world disaster meant nothing whatever in terms of personal happiness. Time passed. I wrote little odds and ends of news and Georges, who, in my mind, was already far away, became my one and only living memory.

I could no longer endure the presence of my parents. I saw in them the obstacle to the future I might build up and, to frighten them and to show them that I was conscious of being twenty, I kept bringing up different projects every day.

" I shall go to Australia and start a publishing house in Melbourne . . ." or else: " I've got a unique opportunity; England will accept two nurses from Kufstein; I could be over there in three weeks' time."

" Are you mad? " asked my mother, as if this were a relevant question.

" No," I answered, " but I shall soon be seeing mad people at close quarters. Apparently, the severe cases wet their beds. . . . I shall write a novel about an asylum over there . . . in English, naturally."

When my father told me I ought to be careful in the little lanes of the camp after dusk, I was over-whelmed by a feeling of despair. Obviously, I should never be able to overcome them. I was imprisoned in the vicious circle of the insane love of parents who no longer had anything to do except to love me. And I wanted to be loved in a different way. I loathed all the details of my childhood that I knew by heart; that I had been adorable, that I had learnt to read when other darling babies, my contemporaries, were only just beginning to walk. My hatred of the piano had

94

turned into a caprice of fate that had prevented the
" infant genius " from becoming a great pianist.
Equally often, I heard how rare it was for a young
girl to be as pure as myself and how very, very careful
I must be not to lose this purity that had been so well
safeguarded! I wanted to scream with rage when
my father made a Latin quotation and I paced round
and round the narrow room like a caged animal. From
sheer despair, I put myself down for a dressmaking
course. But, instead of seeing needles and thread,
I saw a geometrical diagram on the blackboard.
When the teacher, a charming woman, explained that
this parallelogram was none other than the drawing of
a pattern, I promptly made my escape. I had never
had anything but a deep, unsurmountable loathing for
all forms of mathematics!

The miracle, like all miracles, came unexpectedly,
simply and without any fuss. I was vaguely friendly
with a woman in the camp and sometimes took refuge
in her company. She had taught French in Budapest
and she often talked about her youth in Paris and
about the friends who had remained faithful to her.
She was making preparations for her voyage to South
America; she had left Hungary at the same time as
ourselves—towards the end of November 1948. At
my request, she had written to one of her French
friends who lived at Versailles and who, for a long
time, had been looking for a nursery-governess for her
charming little girl of seven.

The letter engaging me arrived one evening at the

end of May. I showed it to my parents with the victorious air of a young Indian brave presenting his first scalp to his elders. My parents found the whole thing impossible, theatrical and ill-considered.

" You want to go and work among total strangers? Heaven knows what a trap may be awaiting you! What you should do, is ask for a scholarship grant and go to the Sorbonne. . . ."

" I can do that over there . . . I don't want to stay here any longer . . . And, besides, why strangers? She knows them very well . . . No, but honestly, I'd rather die than go on like this . . . I want a room whose door is shut by *me* and no one else and where I'll be alone. I want a cupboard with things in it that I've bought out of my own salary. I want to perfect my French . . . I'm fond of children . . . A little girl of seven, that's easy . . . You'll kill me if you keep me here . . . Every generation . . . The rights of youth . . . White slave traffickers have other fish to fry . . . they won't be watching and waiting for *me* . . . But, of course, I'll be careful . . . You simply *must* realise you're being unreasonable . . . A well brought up girl can't be in Paris on her own? In the first place, I shan't be on my own, I shall be looking after a child. Besides, since when have well brought up girls crossed frontiers illicitly without passports? I find that much more shocking, walking on all-fours and being frightened of the moon and of being hunted down by dogs, and crying with your face buried in dead leaves . . . And is it correct for a

96

well-brought up girl to tread on an arm that has come away from a corpse? Come away because it's decomposing ... A well-brought up girl eating horse flesh from horses blown to bits by bombs ... When I was taking my exams in Budapest and I felt someone walking behind me, I shivered with fright. I didn't know what they were tracking me for ... my slim ankles or my bourgeois origin ... What else do you want from me? ... And if these times *are* nothing but danger and suffering, let's go ahead all the same ... But, look here, I'm twenty and a half ... Yes, even the months count ... Heaven knows how long I've been grown-up ... But you know it as well as I do! ... A little girl of seven, it'll be just as if she were my little sister ... In fact, why *haven't* I a little sister?"

I celebrated my liberation by taking the train for Paris. But I was poisoned by all the advice and all those wearisome unproductive conversations. I had used up all my breath during those endless evenings and, once I was actually on the train, my one desire was to leave everything I had known and felt up to that moment, as quickly as possible. My father accompanied me into the compartment; he put the suitcase we had bought in Vienna into the luggage-rack and kissed me. Then he rejoined my mother on the platform. I had still five minutes to get through. I was trembling with feverish impatience; I kept looking at the Kufstein station clock. But, one minute before the hand reached the appointed time, my eyes

97

met the eyes of my parents. And, suddenly over-whelmed with an immense fear and a wild rush of tenderness, I wanted to get out of the train and throw myself into their arms and explain everything, twenty and a half years of love for them—in a single gesture. At that precise moment, my mother's face was lit up by a tearful smile. I think she wanted to tell me, in sixty seconds, everything a mother can tell her daughter who is going off to conquer an infinitesimal corner of the world. My nature was not given to making con-fidences: I was naturally taciturn. It was at my mother's side that I had made the acquaintance of death in Budapest but we never spoke of birth, pain, love and women's secrets. Such reserve was extremely reassuring, and, in the padded shelter of this feigned indifference, I had been able to go calmly through all the crises and the unanswerable questions that beset the transitions from one age to another. This affec-tionate hostility was my refuge and when, in one of Pearl Buck's books, I read the description of the sufferings of a Chinese woman in labour on the fruit-ful earth and encountered, for the first time, that warm atmosphere of blood and tears, it was like my revenge for having crossed that frontier alone and unaided.

. . . But now that the train was slowly beginning to move, my mother walked along beside it. " Be careful, my child," she said, and her face told me that she could have gone on talking to me for hours. My father, too, came up close. " Be *very* careful," he said, in his turn. The train began to move faster and faster. I leant out through the window. They were far away and I shouted: " I love you tremendously, I'll come back soon . . . I love you tremendously. . . ."

Swallowed up by a tunnel, the train gave a death-rattle, and I burst into tears.

# 6

It HAD been arranged that Madame Bruller should meet me at the Gare de l'Est. I had sent her my photo from Kufstein so that she could recognise me easily. But I think that, even without a photo, she would have made no mistake. I had prepared a serious, conscientious nurse's face; the face of a girl who would be attentive to her employer's wishes; in fact, a very correct little person who would not let herself be carried away by her own youth. Rumpled from a sleepless night, my hands damp with stage fright, I watched Paris coming nearer and nearer. The station was swarming with porters; it was almost impossible to avoid them, and I lingered in front of my compartment with my Budapest winter coat over my arm and the cardboard suitcase at my feet. My heart was beating fit to burst my chest and I was convinced I had a black smudge on my forehead for I had been sitting by the window whose frame, in the morning, was covered with a thick layer of soot. I watched the people going past and I was so strung-up by this waiting that I did not notice the young woman who had touched my arm.

" Mademoiselle? "

I said, " How d'you do " with a start.

" My car's in front of the station; come along . . .
Not too tired? "

I answered with a sigh:

" Terribly. Travelling's always. . . ."

But I did not dare go on, for she looked so worried.

" As tired as all that? "

" Oh, but not in the least," I corrected myself.
" Not in the least."

" You know," she said the moment we were in the
car, " the maid had an attack of appendicitis last night;
she was operated on this morning. . . ."

" But I'll help you, madame."

Now that she had mentioned the maid's illness, she
fell silent like someone entirely intent on their driving.

I was sitting beside her and the blinding sun put a
curtain of light between Paris and myself. The
windscreen was dirty and the metallic rays of this unexpected heat were blurred by the layer of dust.
Madame Bruller had an obstinate chin, sharp as a
sarcastic retort, a heavy lipstick, a delicate shiny nose,
eyes fixed on the road in front of her and black hair
drawn into a tight chignon that I longed to touch to
find out if it were real. Without looking at me, she
asked for news of her friend, the teacher.

" She's very well. I think her boat leaves on the
29th for Rio de Janeiro."

Madame Bruller jerked a sentence at me in the
cryptic manner of a dice-player.

" But for her, you wouldn't have been able to come

to us. . . . However, she's given the necessary references."

" I've certainly got a smut somewhere," I thought, " and that smut makes me look suspicious. Otherwise she wouldn't have made that irrelevant remark." I tried to catch a glimpse of myself in the driving-mirror, but without success.

" Where is little Monique? " I asked, risking myself hesitantly on unknown territory. " Is she at school? "

" No. In bed. She's ill. . . . Have you had chicken-pox? "

I just managed not to exclaim: " So she's ill, too! " and said:

" Yes, madame. I had chicken-pox when I was still in Budapest."

She looked at me suddenly; she was able to do so, we were safely on the motor highway.

" In Budapest? "

She said this with so much incredulity that I mechanically touched the little hole beside my ear, invisible to anyone but myself, that the chicken-pox had left me.

" In Budapest? . . ."

After a few moments' silence she went on:

" You'll have quite a lot to do in the first few days. You must stop the child from scratching herself. . . . It itches a great deal."

The tone she used to me was that of a tired teacher repeating the same thing innumerable times to a mental defective. I should have liked to say that chicken-pox itched in Budapest too, but judged it wiser to keep silent.

"I held her little hands all night long; my husband has been sitting up with her for the last two days. . . ."

And the maid, when had that happened? But I did not ask the question.

"I had gloves when I had chicken-pox. . . ."

She shrugged her shoulders:

"It's better to hold her and make sure. . . ."

I had seen the houses of Versailles appearing but, before we arrived in the town itself, she took a by-road and soon we stopped in front of an old, two-storied house. It was covered with ivy and the garden was overgrown with weeds; the wrought-iron gate, rusted by the rain of years, stood half-open. Later, I realised it was impossible to close it.

She opened the front door. The hall was astonishingly small, with two doors to the right, one to the left, and the staircase leading to the upper floor. I put down my coat and my suitcase and followed her. On the first floor there were four bedrooms of which one was occupied by the little invalid and a neighbour who was looking after her, a kindly woman with grey hair.

"Thank you, my dear," said Madame Bruller, bending over the child.

I went up close and I saw a red swollen blotch of a face, completely distorted by a crop of pimples.

"This is Monique, little Monique."

At the sound of her mother's voice, the child let out a yell.

I bent over her and I was aware of the two women watching me keenly. Not a movement, not a sound of my anxious, jerky breathing escaped them. I felt as heavy and clumsy as if they had tied invisible weights to my limbs before I entered the room. I sought the child's eyes. I wanted to feel the first contact which, even if hostile, would be exclusively our own. And if I could make her stop screaming with a smile, I should already have scored a success. I did not love her yet. It is impossible to love out of duty, but I was full of goodwill and, suppressing a spasm of disgust, I lightly touched one of the small hands that was red and damp with saliva. In the distorted face, the eyes were replaced by two slits filled with a black stare, swimming with tears, and the smell of that tortured skin, burning with fever, filled my nostrils and went right down to the bottom of my throat.

The neighbour went on whispering to Madame Bruller. I stood awkwardly by the bed. I must do something or other to please them. I looked in vain for a glass of water I could offer with the classic gesture of nurses. The blanket was well tucked in; there was no point in touching it. The child never stopped moaning; she had placed her voice like an actress who has to keep it up for the five acts to follow. She moaned rhythmically; I hoped one would manage to get accustomed to it, like the tick of a noisy alarm-clock. I sat down on the edge of the bed; the child was quiet from sheer astonishment and the two women slipped out of the room as swiftly and silently as smoke-rings escape from an expert mouth. They had only been waiting for me to sit down, a captive for an unspecified time. When Monique wanted to touch her face, I seized her hands and caught them on the wing. I could not take my eyes off her; her movements were too unexpected. It was hide-and-seek of the reflexes and I was always quicker than she was. The window of the room was scrupulously closed. The curtain let a pale light filter through. I had no watch; the last time I had looked at a clock was at the station. I tried to define the distant noises in the house; downstairs they were opening and shutting doors. A woman's voice—Madame Bruller's perhaps—was speaking on the telephone: I could hear an occasional " Of course," and " Naturally. . . ." I floated in this stifling twilight atmosphere. Monique grew tired before I did; I saw her struggling with a ray of light like a midge on a fly-paper trying to pull off its delicate legs one by one. At last Monique was stuck fast in a kindly sleep; she stopped moaning and, behind the mask of the childish malady, I could see the suffering face that had not even the advantage of charming or moving one by its pallor. I got up and, at last, looked at the room, like a sleepwalker rudely awakened at the very peak of his trance to find himself in his nightclothes on the roof of a five-storied house. This room was fairly large. Beside

the wardrobe, there was a divan; then came a few
toys scattered on some shelves, a chest-of-drawers
with its two bottom drawers open, a locked door, and
a moth-eaten carpet. And, everywhere, in the gilded
shafts of the banished sun, motes of dust danced in
a perpetual ballet; the curtain was not properly
drawn. I tiptoed over to the window. The garden
below was tranquil. A white, silent hen was walking
about and pecking for worms. She plunged her tiny
head into the grass like an unaccustomed bather who
only likes getting wet up to her shoulders.

" Is she asleep? "

Madame Bruller's whispering voice struck me in
the back and took my breath away.

" Yes, she's asleep. . . ."

" Then what are you waiting for? Come and have
lunch, you must be hungry."

I went down with her to the ground floor. The
smell of hot oil and freshly roasted meat filled the
house.

" I'd like to wash my hands."

The request seemed natural to her and she indicated
a door, with an impatient gesture. At last I saw
myself in a glass. I rubbed my hands with a piece of
soap and looked at myself. There was no black smudge
on my forehead but my eyes had dark rings of weariness round them. Those nights of tense waiting at
Kufstein and sixteen hours on the train without any
sleep, made my face look drawn. I cast a furtive
glance round the bathroom. How well I was to come

to know every corner of it! There were two dressing-gowns made of towelling hanging up on hooks. They were worn and weary from too much service; the enamel of the bath was chipped and the geyser bore black traces of flames that were either irregular or over-greedy. On the shelf was a tube of toothpaste, some battered toothbrushes and a pink plastic beaker with the imprint of lips on it. But here, too, there was a window looking out on the garden. I also noticed two pairs of slippers. The man's slippers conjured up the thought of Monsieur Bruller. He must exist and, judging from his slippers, he was tall and heavy; a hundred kilogrammes of malice bundled into a striped jacket. I imagined him as fat and over-whelming. I emerged from the bathroom and Madame Bruller led me into the dining-room where a thin, frail man was reading a paper that lay on his plate.

" This is Christine," said Madame and I felt a certain disquiet that she did not add the exact defini-tion: " Christine, the nurse." Reduced to being only Christine, the horizon of diverse tasks seemed to me vast, almost limitless.

" Did you have a good journey? "

Monsieur held out his small soft hand to me as he asked the question. But he did not wait for my reply and plunged back into his newspaper.

Madame Bruller indicated my place, as if she were showing me a town she wanted to present to me.

" You're going to eat with us, like one of the

family. . . . Would you mind putting your paper down, darling?"

The man did not stir. The new tone she had adopted on my account was so unexpected that her husband had not even realised that she was speaking to him.

" Your paper. . . ."

Her true voice struck him like the explosion of a bomb. He put it down by his plate and we attacked a stew, accompanied by boiled potatoes.

" Would you bring the salt, Christine? "

I stood up.

" Where is the kitchen? "

" The door on the left. You'll find it on the table."

The kitchen was in a disastrous state. A regiment of saucepans was piled up on the floor along with plates, cutlery and glasses, a whole bridal dowry, complete with the wedding presents! The fleeting ghost of the maid gave me an outsize grin; it had the impertinence of beings who have never existed. I found the salt. The Brullers looked at me. They wanted to see my reaction to the vision of the kitchen printed on my face. They pressed round me as poor relations press round the doctor who is watching over the last moments of the rich aunt on her death bed. I pretended to have seen nothing.

" You left Hungary when? "

" Seven months ago."

Madame Bruller inquired:

" So late? Why did you wait till 1948? "

Monsieur Bruller did not want to be left out.

" Must be no joke, what's going on over there. . . ."

" Oh no. . . ."

" Were you in Budapest all the time? "

" Up to taking my Higher Certificate."

" It's all so dreadfully sad," went on Madame Bruller, then added:

" You'll help me wash up after lunch, won't you? "

" Of course, madame.  With pleasure."

Monsieur Bruller said pleasantly:

" I did not think Hungarian girls were fair.  I imagined them with long black plaits, sometimes right down to their ankles."

" It's rather unusual," I replied evasively.

They left the table very hurriedly.  Madame Bruller had explained to me that she would take advantage of the child's sleep to snatch a little rest. . . .

" My husband is going back to his office in Paris . . . I'll leave you on your own . . . You'll find all the cleaning things you need . . . Afterwards, I'll show you your room . . . But during these next few difficult days, you'll sleep on the divan in the child's room . . ."

I heard Monsieur's car start up and I was left helpless on this raft, floating on a sea of ill-kept lawn. How far away Paris was!  " Write to us at once," my mother had said. . . .  " The very day you arrive! "

In the silent house, abandoned in the midst of

mountains of dirty crockery, I felt I was living in a dream from which I could waken at will. But it was no use thinking. I must begin to collect the necessary things for the washing-up. I heated the water in a clothes-copper. I found a brush but it was very worn-out and was shedding its bristles as a sick dog sheds its hair. I had to heat up three lots of water to vanquish the pile of washing-up. When everything was sparkling, and at the very moment when I had an irresistible desire to sit down, Madame Bruller called me:

" Christine, come here, quick. . . ."

I ran: she called down from the floor above:

" Would you make me some very weak tea and some warm milk for Monique? "

After that monster cleaning-up, I already knew where to find tea and milk . . . and despair.

Till evening, it was a constant whirlwind of orders.

" Christine, would you mind airing the bedroom? I've taken the blanket off the bed, you might make it up again. . . . If you've got a minute, then do wash Monique's little bits and pieces that I've put in a heap in the bathroom; as a rule, I send everything to the laundry, but the child's nightgowns are too fragile. . . . Don't you think there's a lot of dust in the living-room? . . . If you're used to having *goûter*, do get yourself some. . . .

I began with Monsieur's and Madame's bed. It was the first time I had seen a vast French bed and Madame told me to tuck the blankets in smoothly and tightly. To begin with I stripped off everything and removed the imprints of the two bodies, the lean one and the flabby one, united in the holy bonds of matrimony. Madame decided that the sheets were dirty already and gave me some clean ones. I perceived that she had decided to make a fresh start in life and " put everything in order at last." Monique moaned again; her voice was fresh, full of vigour and expression. The enormous mattress confronted me like a warrior, heavy when I lifted it but becoming horribly pliable when I wanted to master it. It was impossible to turn it; it remained bent double on the bed like a giant with stomach-ache. But at last I succeeded and the room was soon tidy. During a minute when Madame had her eye off me, I glanced out into the garden and I saw the hen just in front of the window; her head was bent over to the right as she stared at an invisible point; her white feathers looked yellow in the twilight; she wore her delicate red comb like a diadem. She raised her head towards me and her eyes seemed full of kindly curiosity, and, to show her favour, she winked her left eye, drawing up her eyelid from below. We looked at each other; we were already accomplices and I decided I would call her Undine. In her knowing silence, she was like a fairy on the dark green grass.

" Christine, what are you doing? "

What, in fact, *was* I doing? Nothing. And I answered, like my own echo:

" Nothing, Madame."

" Are you tired? "

" A little, madame."

" Come along, we must go and get dinner ready.
My husband will be home in half an hour."

Before going down to the ground floor I went into
Monique's bedroom. She was sitting propped up
against her pillows and reading a child's picture-book.

" Will you tell me a story? "

I would gladly have stayed but Madame was already
impatient.

" Christine, aren't you coming? "

" Stay here," whimpered Monique; " Tell me a
story."

Monique howled: I went downstairs and Madame
said:

" You mustn't make a child in that state cry."

" I didn't mean to make her cry. She called me
and I went into her room. She wanted me to tell her
a story."

Madame Bruller became severe.

" You mustn't spoil her. Whatever you do, don't
spoil her. . . ."

I laid the table. I peeled unknown vegetables,
great menacing black roots. Madame gave me a
chance to escape.

" When you go out of the house, turn right and go
round to the back—you'll find a cage. We have a
hen who lays an egg every day—that's Monique's
egg."

I was enchanted and I went out of the house with a

great sigh of relief. The little street in front of it was deserted; the shadows were already lengthening under the trees; the warm air caressed my face. I found the cage beside two bushes covered with buds. The little cage was open and on the yellow straw I saw a dazzlingly white egg; I touched it, it was warm; Undine could not be far away. She appeared, with her crooked diadem, swaying as she walked. I held out some crumbs to her on the palm of my hand; she looked at them with interest but was still too hesitant to accept them and retired into her cage as if into a sedan chair. I closed the little door and went back to the house with the egg.

Dinner was anything but tranquil. I had to go upstairs twice to Monique and afterwards I hurriedly swallowed the food that had gone cold on my plate. Madame gave me some sheets and, feeling extremely depressed, I made up my bed on the divan in Monique's room. How much I should have liked a room to myself! But perhaps, in a few days, I should have the maid's since they now no longer even mentioned her.

I had no dressing-gown so I had to dress again completely in the bathroom to walk the few steps to Monique's bedroom. With the aid of a sedative, she had gone to sleep again and Madame said I had been extraordinarily lucky to have arrived at the end of this disagreeable illness.

Monsieur came home very late. I heard the brakes of his car in a troubled half-sleep. My blanket was too short and I had to double myself up to keep warm.

The pillow exhaled a faint, almost imperceptible smell of mildew. From where had she unearthed that pillow for me? I went to sleep with my knees huddled up. I was too weary to cry.

Sharing the intimate life of other people is terrible. After I had been there four weeks, I knew their faces, the words they used, the way they walked that deformed their slippers, the peevish mood that dominated the morning, the insipid taste of their cooking. Monique, convalescent now, displayed a face that was pale once more and stared insistently at me with her large eyes during meals. She expressed openly what her parents dared not say; she had full liberty, since she was only a child. I do not say she hated me; her feeling about me was something subtler and more refined. She would stare at me coldly; she would burst into yells and tears, and then be suddenly silent, awaiting her opportunity.

"Why have you got an accent? Is Hungary like China? Why do you have meals with us? The maids always had theirs in the kitchen. . . ."

The father would intervene, as diplomat and humanist:

"But, Monique, you know quite well Christine isn't a maid, she's your nurse."

Monique was not embarrassed.

"Up to now I didn't have a nurse, only a maid. . . . Why do you call her something else?"

"You talk too much, child," said the mother.

" Eat up your food nicely and then Christine will put you to bed."

Putting her to bed was a struggle over every single article of clothing she wore. Unbuttoning her innumerable jerseys and undoing her shoe laces were major operations. To perform them, I knelt down in front of her. I also told stories; I told them very badly; I yawned as soon as I began a story. It's not my fault, but children's stories bore me to death. If only I could talk about Wanda! . . . Wanda will have a Negro lover. . . .

" Is it nice to have a lover? " But my mother's menacing face banished the word " lover "; I purified my thoughts and asked myself the question again: " Is it nice to have a husband? "

" Oh do hurry up and begin," Monique would say.

" Once upon a time. . . ."

I imagined Georges in his silver mine. I saw him walking up to his ankles in the liquid silver that ran like an underground river.

" If you don't tell me a story, I shall tell Mamma."

" What shall you tell Mamma, my precious? " inquired Madame Bruller, appearing in the doorway, her face covered with thick cream and her hair tied up in a scarf. Her face was so shiny that her features had lost their definition; nose, eyebrows and mouth were all blurred under the oily mask. Her dressing-gown was open a little at the neck; she was already in her nightdress. I could hear Monsieur Bruller bustling to and fro. The sight of his wife almost made me pity him. Kissing her must be like kissing a lump of lard!

"But, Christine, you've no imagination! The poor little thing's *so* fond of fairy-tales. . . ."

At last, they had all gone to bed. To-morrow they would have a long lie-in and *I* should be free. To-morrow, Sunday, I was going to Paris. Apparently there was a special Mass for the Hungarians. Since I had been there, I hadn't had a Sunday to myself, and, to-morrow, I was going to have a whole day. I would leave at nine so as to arrive in time for the eleven o'clock Mass.

# 7

I woke up very early and had to wait, lying perfectly still, for the hours to pass. At night, by Madame Bruller's orders, the windows were hermetically sealed for she had an almost hysterical fear of burglars and draughts. Towards dawn, the house was always full of the stuffy smell of heavy sleep. I got up about half-past seven and tiptoed to the bathroom; I shuddered with apprehension when the gurgling of the tap sounded very loud. I turned it down to a very thin trickle of water and shut the door with infinite precaution. At last, I left it all behind me, and went out to take Undine some drinking-water. She was standing on one of her yellow feet, with her head tucked under her wing; when she saw me, she shook herself and avidly pecked the crumbs from my palm. I had the feeling that her pecks were sharp, affectionate little kisses, a manifestation of primeval sympathy, a sign from that other world beyond the human one. That morning, everything was reaching out expectantly to a new awakening of life. The buds, all those tight green little knots, had unfolded during the night and the frail young leaves were scattered with dewdrops.

I set off in the direction of the station. I was wearing a little blue woollen dress and my hair hung loose on my shoulders: the Kufstein missal was so big that I could not shut my handbag. The late June sun was already hot and the sleepers of Versailles would be throwing off their blankets in their feverish doze. I imagined the families behind the closed shutters. But none of them had the faces of Monsieur or Madame Bruller. With a logical, conscious tenacity, I wanted to preserve that image of France I had made for myself years ago. I knew that Monsieur and Madame were no more than a disagreeable detail. The day before, I had sent a letter to my parents, a restrained letter, expressed with considerable reserve: " I am very well and I am glad to be in France."

Moreover, I was always thrilled when, as " sender," I could inscribe Versailles on the back of the envelope. Not for a fortune would I have admitted that the crazy rhythm of my work had prevented me up to now from seeing the palace, the gardens and the shade of Marie-Antoinette whom I loved on account of Fersen. Even when one is a Republican, one forgives all in a queen who had the capacity to love. It was Stefan Zweig who had told me all I knew about her and told it with infinite art, at once compassionate and indiscreet. Stefan Zweig's book on Marie-Antoinette had seemed to me like the literary speech for the defence of a barrister who was in love with his client and was no longer bound by professional secrecy.

That morning, the dead streets of Versailles were

embalmed by a youthful, radiant sun. I walked in silence and a golden haze. I caught the train at the last minute and, leaning back against the hard wooden seat, I was overwhelmed with inexplicable terror. I was going to see Paris. How I should have loved to see it in different circumstances—with a passport in order in my pocket, a blue beret on my head, a portable typewriter in my hand and a book of traveller's cheques in my handbag! When I was building up my plans in Budapest, that was how I had imagined arriving in Paris.

When I gave up my ticket at the barrier, I realised, that very instant, that my hands were rough and my nails broken. I did too much washing and scrubbing in Madame's kitchen with products that were cruel to the skin. In the waiting room, I saw the map of the métro. I went straight down into it, without going out into the street, like a swimmer who goes faster under water. The kindly women ticket-collectors helped me to find the place on the Left Bank where the church was situated. I left the métro and found myself in front of the building and, crossing a courtyard, I went into a chapel that was still empty.

I knelt down on a prie-dieu, and, with my chin on my piously-clasped hands, I observed the people who were coming in in little groups and dispersing themselves in the nave. A smell of cold incense floated in the air and I felt that, in a few minutes, I should be very hungry indeed; I had left Versailles without having any breakfast.

I was extremely distracted during the religious service; I only caught a few words of the sermon in Hungarian: "Be good, hard-working and kind." And, after that, I plunged back into my own thoughts like someone falling into unconsciousness. Towards the end, I went out into the little courtyard where my compatriots were already chatting. Later, I realised that this was the regular meeting-place where they saw each other once a week. I did not know a soul. I waited aimlessly in a corner, simply to pass a little time and, suddenly, something gave me a shock as violent as that of the first pain that heralds an illness. I caught sight of Georges with another young man. In the sunlight that flooded the courtyard, he was slim, elegant and transparently pale but the expression of his face betrayed great weariness. The fair-skinned face was no longer tanned by the heat of Peru. I looked at him for three or four minutes before he saw me. With an incredulous smile, racking his memory for my name, he came up to me, paralysed at the sight of someone resuscitating from a forgotten past, and held out his hand.

" How d'you do. . . ."

A brief silence and he added, uncertainly:

" Christine. . . ."

" How d'you do, Georges. . . . Didn't you go to Peru? What happened to the silver mine? "

He made an embarrassed little grimace.

" The mine? It's flooded."

Suddenly all the details of Georges's good or evil

fortunes seemed so close and familiar that I exclaimed:
"Oh! Poor Georges. . . ."

"It's not so serious as all that," he replied and added almost at once: "Can I come with you, wherever you're going? . . . And, by the way, how do you come to be in Paris? You had difficulties in Innsbruck. . . ."

We left the courtyard of the church. The street was already bustling, but I caught sight of a café. Seeing an Italian Espresso coffee apparatus through the window, I thought, if I could get as far as one of the little tables, I should be saved.

"You do walk fast," said Georges, smiling, and I crossed the street without looking right or left.

"I'd like to have a coffee, now this minute. . . ."

He took hold of my elbow to guide me and this gesture produced a curious reaction: the left half of my body, on his side, turned burning hot; the other half, the right, became cold, objective and full of suspicion. At last, seated at a tiny table and nibbling a *croissant*, I looked him in the eyes. His eyes frequently changed colour; the iris turned blue, grey or green according to the play of light. Then I drank my longed-for coffee with considerable difficulty; I would have liked to hide my ruined hands. . . .

"Yes, all alone."

I heard my own voice: "And you too?"

"Absolutely alone; my parents stayed in Hungary."

123

" And now that you're not going to Peru after all, what are your plans? "

" I've put myself down for a course in International Law . . . and later on . . ."

He took out a cigarette and I noticed the signet-ring on his left hand.

He was aware of my glance at the ring and excused himself, saying:

" Oh, I don't always wear it, you know.  I don't like it. . . .  And what about you?  What do you want to do in Paris? "

" Write."

I was genuinely astonished by my own admission, as if I had begun to speak in a language hitherto unknown to me.

" What do you want to write? "

" Novels, lots of novels—and short stories."

He drank the last mouthful of his coffee.

" Do you know any Paris publishers? "

" Me?  Paris publishers?  I don't know a soul in Paris and I'm working in Versailles.  I'm a little girl's nurse. . . ."

After a long walk, we reached the banks of the Seine.

" I'll show you Paris," he said.

But I shook my head.

" Not yet, later on. . . ."

How could I have told him about my resentments and my obscure troubles, about that feverish little rebellion that made me hostile and unjust towards

124

Paris? How could I explain this life I had to lead, this working from morning to night? How could I tell him that it would have been better if he had gone off to Peru because I was already attached to him? My loneliness was too great not to fall in love at once; there was an empty, hungry place in my heart that I was preparing as carefully as a mistress of a house expecting a guest. . . .

" But I *shall* show you Paris all the same," he said, with charming insistence.

I looked at the Seine; I pretended to be lost in my thoughts but nothing could have been falser; I was observing him and I was observing myself. How easy it all was for fate; two lonely young people meeting in Paris; the quay from which a fisherman was casting his line in the water; the pair of lovers kissing on the steps. They were sipping each other's lips—as if they were tasters and we were kings, and they were proving to us the wine was not poisoned. No, my friend, I don't want all that; it would be a love affair too scientifically prepared; the sky is too blue; the air is too charged with spring already ripening into summer! . . .

" You're not listening to me. . . . I was saying that Octave Aubry was right when . . ."

. . . And, once again, for the last time, I made a final effort to detach myself. I went through all the things I had heard about love. And, besides, a fair person should never love another fair person.

I turned towards him to say good-bye and, suddenly,

my throat went tight with emotion. He was handsome and anxious, tense and serious.

I replied:

" Yes . . . Yes, we can see each other again next
Sunday. . . ."

I had the feeling that this day would last for ever.
There was no more Versailles, no more Monique, no
more suburban train. There was nothing but a vague,
shy love. . . .

# 8

MY LIFE at Versailles had the imperturbable rhythm of an hour-glass. The hours dribbled on from morning to night without a moment's rest. I did not like Madame Bruller's shrill, urgent orders so I hurried to anticipate them. It was an appalling rush; I had the entire house on my hands. In the morning, I got up first and prepared the breakfast; then I went up to wake Monique who was invariably sulky and invariably ready to invent ways of irritating me, with a cistern of tears behind her black eyes. Madame Bruller came down to the dining-room tottering with sleep and bowed under the weight of her dreams. Monsieur Bruller nervously fingered the razor-cuts on his cheek and examined his bloodstained handkerchief with the slow intentness of a schoolboy. While Madame Bruller was doing the shopping, I cleaned the house, while keeping an eye on Monique, who, thanks to the school holidays, spent her days in the garden. The despairing cries of Undine frequently made me descend with a broom in my hand. One day, Monique faced up to me.

" Leave me alone, it's *my* hen."

" But I don't allow you to torture her," I replied fiercely.

She almost hissed the threat at me:

" Mamma said she's going to boil the hen. She doesn't lay any more."

It was only too true that Undine was tired and languid. For the past week, I had looked in vain for her egg. She clucked in a lost way and turned her head to the right, looking at me with a puzzled expression and displaying her red eyelid like a tiny shutter. But I had never suspected that her life was in peril. During my animated conversation with Monique, she had escaped and vanished behind a bush.

I went upstairs again and resumed my perpetual motion. The bed with its stale warmth, the windows I flung open, the objects I gave life to in my imagination—I decided that each had a soul. And now the comb stuffed with Madame Bruller's black hairs would groan: " How disgusting . . ." and the down-at-heel slippers whimper: " You'd think they were camels or elephants. . . ." Madame Bruller shivered in the well-aired house. " What a draught! " " Madame, we're in July." " But the child will get earache . . ." I said not another word; I shut the windows, singing a tune in my own mind of which the words ran: " It's all so stupid, I'll get away. . . ."

Madame took the only deck-chair in the house and lay in the sun; her face anointed with grease and her arms hanging inert. I was almost certain that she had never given herself to her husband with such voluptuous sensuality.

I finished cooking the lunch about one o'clock,

128

when Monsieur arrived. He ground the brakes of his car and *I* wanted to grind my teeth. I waited at table and, when I was able to sit down, I pecked at my food; I was too tired to feel hungry. I carried the coffee out into the garden; they had retired into the shade: " You know it's so dangerous, a full sun on a full stomach! " I went in again to wash up and scraps of conversation floated in through the open kitchen window. Without their having told me so directly, I knew that the villa at the seaside had been rented from the first of August.

" A real rest . . . Absolute peace and quiet . . ."

Monsieur's voice promised marvels as he built up castles in Spain.

" You don't even think about the cooking. But, of course, Christine will be pleased—the air's so good there. . . ."

To-morrow, I would tell them my decision. To-day, I was still a slave, but to-morrow they would know that the bird was about to fly.

If I had had time to lie down for one minute, I should have fallen asleep straight away. I pined for a long, dreamless sleep, a semblance of death. I trembled with fatigue and I started whenever I heard Madame's voice. After doing the washing-up, I got the *goûter* ready. After *goûter*, I took Monique for a walk. " The poor little thing's been shut up all day." She adored running off and disappearing into corners; I ran after her, panting. I had learnt to weep without shedding tears. I swallowed my tears;

129

they burnt my throat and left a bitter taste on my palate. When I caught Monique, I gripped her hand firmly in mine. "Ow, you're hurting me," she cried. But I did not answer; I went on walking, with my knees shaking under me.

When we returned, I began to prepare the dinner. Madame Bruller came into the kitchen; she sat down on a chair and looked at me.

"We're soon going to the sea, Christine. You won't look so pale down there. . . . By the way, why are you so pale? I hope there's nothing the matter with you. I can't help worrying, because of the child."

I peeled the old potatoes; they were bluish and withered and full of "eyes." Madame Bruller leant her elbows on the table and flung a sentence at me that was like a signal for the hounds to tear their quarry to pieces.

"To-morrow, Sunday, I'm going to boil the hen. She's very fat, she'll make a good thick stew. My husband adores that."

I went on peeling potatoes without looking at the executioner's face. On Sunday morning, I was going away for ever.

That night, after dinner, I had permission to have a bath. I locked myself into the bathroom and, as soon as I was naked, I looked at my back. It was thin and narrow and the salient shoulder-blades looked like weights attached to my shoulders.

For two months I had been living like some monstrous hostess who adores having people round her and has invited an entire family to stay in her cottage. My guests were Monsieur and Madame Bruller and their daughter Monique. I had looked after them well, but it was over; I was leaving to-morrow morning. With two months' salary in my pocket, I would rent a tiny room and I would look for some other work.

Someone knocked at the door.

" How much longer are you going to be? "

" Just coming, madame."

In my bed I doubled myself up as I did every night. Monique made me get up again to give her a glass of water.

When they were all asleep I thought things over. I could not return to Kufstein. I wanted to stay in Paris; I *must* stay there. I would easily find another job. My body ached with weariness and sleep would not come. My thoughts were lit up by a terrifying lucidity, an intellectual aurora borealis. It was impossible to keep one single dark corner in my soul. What was the good of lying to others or to oneself? Georges would be waiting for me to-morrow at the Gare Saint-Lazare as usual. And our meeting to-morrow would be decisive.

The heat of that house was stifling me. I felt dazed, hovering between dream and reality. I threw off the blanket as I might have pushed away an old dog lying on my feet. The mildewed smell of my pillow was insidiously suffocating me. Motionless and lethargic, I felt the sweat trickling down my back and loneliness gnawed at me like a relentless pain.

With burning eyes, I waited for the dawn and, as soon as it began to be light, I got up and dressed. I sat down, fully dressed, on the edge of my bed and, about seven o'cock, I picked up the cardboard suitcase. It had served me as a wardrobe for two months. I left the house, shutting the door carefully behind me. I made my way to Undine's cage. She was lying on her straw; I woke her up. She fluffed up her battered feathers and wanted to protect her invisible eggs; she was broody. I chased her out of her cage but she did not understand and kept lying down every five steps with an indignant cluck. I whispered:

" You're a fool; she'll kill you if you stay here. . . ."

But Undine, in the grip of her obstinate maternal instinct, kept lying down in front of me; she wanted to hatch those invisible eggs. I grabbed hold of her and the sickly heat of her body burnt my arm. I left the wrought-iron gate wide open. In a little street near the station, I had often seen an old lady cleaning out her canary's cage at the window. She would certainly not roast *her* bird when it stopped singing. With Undine clutched under my arm, I walked fast and I deposited her in front of the old lady's closed door.

Half an hour later I took the train to Paris.

# 9

It would have been better if, from the very beginning, I had had the courage to admit that my marriage was a failure. But the first year of it left me no time for analysis. Now that I can see it in perspective and so judge it objectively, I can re-create in myself the rhythm of that past unhappiness—the first kiss and the first blow, the first false smile and the long, disturbing silences that often fell between us.

I can still see myself arriving at the Gare Saint-Lazare. He was waiting for me on the platform, with a bunch of flowers in his hand. He took my case, and we went to his quiet little hotel in Passy. I had clothed him with so many qualities that I was like a designer who had run wild and in a fever of enthusiasm, so overdressed a wax doll that, in the end, the doll had melted and she was left with empty hands. I never stopped interpreting his words and his gestures, and, with a monstrous egotism, I distorted everything. I wanted to live with a hero and I had made up my mind that the father of my children would be a world celebrity; for example, a barrister whose speeches would make a public sensation. I was completely taken aback when he told me one day that the law did not interest him in the slightest; however it was only for a moment that my obdurate will slackened.

" But what *would* you like to do? "

Before he answered, he lit a cigarette and, through the smoke, his face looked pure, almost childlike.

" I always wanted to be an engineer."

" But that's marvellous," I exclaimed. I could already see his hand pressing the button that would start up the machinery of a dam that would bring prosperity to an entire country.

" That's out," he said in self-defence. " Being an engineer was only a boy's dream. . . . I'd like to become an architect."

And, already, I was admiring him as if he were Le Corbusier.

I ought to have been more indulgent and more sincere; I ought to have abandoned that atmosphere of dreamy optimism I myself had created.

So my loneliness persisted and, when I woke up beside him for the first time, I felt that everything had changed, except myself. I emerged from that night cruelly lucid and utterly stupefied. I could no longer understand Madame Bovary. Had she really gone to Rouen twice a week for *that*?

That morning, Georges took me to the Eiffel Tower. He wanted me to have a complete view of Paris. The lift was too expensive for our very meagre purse and Georges told me we were going up on foot by the staircase. I raised my head and looked up at the

gigantic tower with utter despair. I was terribly
thirsty and I felt a scorching pain at every step.

I did not want to disappoint him, we knew each
other so little. He gazed enthusiastically at the tower,
his eyes shining, and added:

" I only like sporting women. . . ."

" I'm very thirsty."

Had Madame Bovary been thirsty too?

" You shall have a drink up there. On the third-
story platform, you shall have a nice bottle of Coca-
Cola. . . . Come on, courage! . . ."

My high pointed heels tapped on the steps like
the beak of a woodpecker searching for grubs. I held
on to the iron rail and I had to keep up the same
rhythm without ever slowing down for Georges
followed on my heels without giving me a moment's
respite. As the Champ-de-Mars became smaller and
smaller, I forced myself not to look to right or left,
but that enormous flayed animal which is the Eiffel
Tower presented nothing to my eyes but its iron veins
and muscles and arteries and, on either side, above
and below, sheer emptiness. The sky that brooded
over this folly vacillated; so did the tiled or slated
roofs; the chimneys seemed to sway in the wind; I
could no longer see the tower except as a loathsome
giraffe, stretching its stiff, interminable neck up into
the clouds and holding a bottle of Coca-Cola in its
parched mouth! At last we arrived at a platform. . . .
I have no idea whether it was the fourth or the fifth.
I had the feeling that I had been turning round ever

since I was born and that I should go on turning round in my coffin like a brainless top that someone starts spinning again with a flick of the hand every time it wants to totter to a stop. I did not know that I should go on revolving like that during the six years to come, that I should go on spinning on my own axis, always humming the same music, the same monotonous tune. . . .

On one of the platforms he took me towards the edge.

The tower itself began to tremble. I thought the wind was going to carry us away. Below, appallingly far away, in another world, was that the distant earth or the nearby moon? I no longer knew. I saw the lines of motor-cars flowing towards the great arteries, the tiny bridges over the miniature river and the houses that were no bigger than stooks of corn in a wheatfield.

I heard Georges's voice explaining to me:

" Over there you can see Notre Dame, the Panthéon, the Île Saint-Louis and the Palais de Chaillot. . . ."

A bitter resentment made me shut my eyes.

I did not want to see this inaccessible Paris, this Paris that was so perfectly clear and mapped-out and conceived for foreigners. Seized by a giddiness that made my stomach heave and clutching frantically on to Georges's arm, I imagined someone in one of those houses . . . those doll's houses manufactured for an enormous toy-shop. I imagined a man alone in his room, reciting a poem to himself in a very low voice so as to keep himself company with his own words.

Fascinated, I turned to Georges and shouted in the wind:

" Do you like poems ? "

" Not much," he answered. . . . " But, I say, do look at Paris! . . ."

At last, we were able to descend and, from below, I gave the tower one last malevolent glance like a sick person who had just had a dangerous operation being shown the erring appendix in a jam-jar.

We drank a bottle of Coca-Cola at the bottom; the bar at the top was closed. My weak legs trembled under the table. Georges, gay and happy, leant across and asked me a question:

" Are you tired, darling ? "

I would have liked to burst into an energetic, sporting reply, full of tireless enthusiasm, but I was aware of a grain of pride in his voice, the glow of an accomplished feat that leaves a pleasant, intimate memory of satisfaction. His voice was tinged with an astonishing male arrogance. He was thinking of our night and my own mind was entirely occupied with those endless stairs.

" Yes, I'm very tired," I admitted weakly, and I withdrew my right foot from my shoe without his noticing. I barricaded myself behind my eyelids whose long lashes aided and abetted me and I wedged my limp shoulders against the back of the uncomfortable little chair. It was an easy, kindly lie, a lie that had no apparent consequences. A lie that I launched like a ping-pong ball against the heights of that tower and which I knew would not rebound with a smart tap on my head. And, besides, I had to remember that Georges was my life-companion; I belonged to him, body and soul. I must not complicate the whole future by thinking too much. That night I went to sleep with burning feet and an aching body, but with a quiet mind.

# 10

We loved each other deeply through the medium of our common memories of Hungary. He described the bedroom he had had as a boy; it had had a flowered curtain and the light walls were always sunlit. I talked about our library, about my school on the hill of Rozsadomb, about my parents whom I now loved more than ever, about my uncle whose handwriting was the same as his. We had made plans for our entire life and he replied evasively to his parents' letters urging him to go off to Australia. The beginning of that autumn was dazzlingly warm and bright. Sometimes we strolled hand in hand through that old quarter of Passy. His parents, anxious about our future, would have liked us to have already left Europe as far behind as possible. Mine, especially my mother, kept insisting on a religious marriage.

Before taking up my new post as a governess which a Christian organisation had procured for me, I consulted the list of Paris publishers that Georges had copied out for me from a professional telephone directory at the post office. Through my compatriots, I had learnt that, at one of the big publishing houses, there was a Hungarian reader who advised for or against the manuscripts that were sent in.

I went to this address on a peaceful afternoon when Paris was still calm and somnolent. The office I was looking for was in a sunless cul-de-sac. I rang for a long time at the big, ancient door. The building had a deserted look. I stood waiting, with my heart thumping and my twelve short stories in a green folder. At last, footsteps. . . . A man opened the door.

" What do you want, mademoiselle? "

" Good afternoon. . . . Could I speak to the Hungarian reader? "

He looked at me without curiosity.

" You're Hungarian? "

" Yes. . . . Is he in? "

His eyes glanced from my face to the green folder.

" You've brought a manuscript? "

" Yes. Is he in, the reader? "

" The office is still closed, mademoiselle, but you can come in for a minute. The Literary Director's secretary happens by chance to be in. . . . Go up to the first floor, it's the second door on the left."

The ground floor to which he admitted me was bathed in darkness and I saw, heaped up on a vast counter, great piles of books. Everything smelt of mildew, like my pillow at Versailles; there was a smell of old yellowed papers, covered with fine dust, like the smell in our loft at home in Budapest. The commissionaire followed me, faithful and silent, like a big dog who is in the habit of accompanying his master to the cemetery. I turned towards him but I did not dare ask him whether they had any living authors too or whether this was only a waxwork museum, a monument to the frailty of human thought.

I knocked on the door he had indicated.

" Come in! " replied an astonished voice.

A woman with greying hair and a fleeting smile raised her head from behind a large desk and looked at me, her eyes full of question-marks.

" Who are you, mademoiselle, and how did you manage to get in here? "

She was surprised but not hostile.

" Good afternoon, madame. It was the commissionaire who told me you were here. I've heard that you have a Hungarian reader here and I've brought a manuscript."

I held the manuscript out to her over the desk but she did not touch it, as if she were unwilling to commit herself by any rash gesture.

" What is it? "

I tucked my file under my arm again.

" Some short stories . . . twelve short stories. . . ."

She was not in the least impressed by their number and told me to sit down.

During the first moment of silence, while she was studying me, I waited for the questions about my nationality, the exact date of my leaving Hungary; perhaps she would even want my fingerprints.

" We have no Hungarian reader, mademoiselle. There's some mistake. Who could have misinformed you like that? "

How could I explain about the courtyard of the church and the information we exchanged after Mass?

Already on my feet I asked her the direct question:

" You don't know where I could get my short stories read? "

She gave a kindly smile—exactly the smile one gives a baby who absolutely insists on walking but falls over at every step because its legs cannot support the weight of its body.

" You know, it's difficult with short stories. You can't sell short stories . . . at least, not unless you're an author like Maupassant. . . . What might interest us would be a short novel . . . packed with incident —modern—full of life. . . ."

I nearly screamed:

" You want a novel? "

And I saw the deliciously impertinent shade of Wanda appear before my eyes and sit down in the arm-chair beside the desk.

She was extremely affable.

" Why, certainly, mademoiselle. Write a novel and, when you've finished it, bring it to us. . . ."

I saw from her face that she was convinced she had got rid of me for ever. She did not know that, with the invisible Wanda, there were three of us in the office.

I said good-bye to her and, at the door, I turned my head towards her and added:

" I'll come back in three months with my novel. Will that suit you? "

Determined to be patient to the end of this scene which she obviously regarded as a frivolity one could allow oneself during the last days of the holidays, she replied:

" You mustn't hurry yourself too much; come whenever you're ready. . . ."

I went down by the back stairs. The man was placidly waiting for me below. I glanced discreetly at the books; they were not cut; they had grown old, still keeping their secrets like books closed for ever.

" Why are there so many books here? "

The commissionaire shrugged his shoulders and answered in one word:

" Stocktaking."

I pressed him further.

" And after stocktaking they'll be sent to bookshops. So you *will* sell them after all, won't you? "

" *Sell* them? "

The sacrilegious word exploded like a tear-gas bomb. The man carefully blew his nose and, instead of answering me, sneezed several times.

He accompanied me to the door and, by way of farewell, he said:

" It's very hard to sell books. Very hard. . . ."

I found myself once more in the sunset light and the warmth of that late August day as if in another world. I was excited and happy at my first contact with literary life.

I passed a small terrace that encroached on part of the pavement and sat down on a little chair at a table no bigger than a plate. The tired waiter brought me a coffee with a faintly disdainful expression; all round me was an orgy of beers and pineapple-juices. I contemplated the passers-by with a shy, profound happiness. I was trying to find the first words of my novel, the phrase that would arrest the readers' attention. I wanted to avoid landscapes, skyscapes and analyses; I would have liked to fling down some brutal, unexpected action on the paper. I sipped my coffee lazily and I was depressed at the thought of having to begin working for other people again. But nothing could stop the flow of ideas. Wanda was present to me; I could already see her on a road in a snowstorm, abandoned, with a child on her hands, near a frontier that she had to cross illicitly. If I had three months' freedom I could write my novel. . . . But what did it matter? I would write it just the same in someone else's house, during the night . . . or at dawn. . . .

In the métro, the vision of that cemetery of books returned to me, but I comforted myself: " Even the most meagre thought must surely become nobler after such a long wait! "

When I saw Georges again and told him all about my afternoon I asked him outright:

" Do you think a writer can live by his books? "

" Why, of course," he answered. " Look at Margaret Mitchell, for example. . . ."

# II

THE FIRST MOMENT I saw the house at Garches, I forgot all about my distress at leaving Paris. Georges had remained behind at the little hotel hunting for work. Every day he cut out advertisements offering various jobs. I arrived at Garches one Monday, knowing I should not see him again until Sunday.

Under the spell of some indefinable charm I walked fearlessly up the path that led to the house through a garden whose fragile beauty was at the mercy of the first slightly harsher wind. Autumn was entrenching itself behind the full-blown roses; I only brushed them with my eyes, wanting to preserve the petals whose edges were already browned. The still supple stems carried the blossoms with the modest strength of young bodies unashamed of their ageing heads.

The big door opening on the white paved hall was open; I crossed the threshold timidly but, when I found myself in front of a glass that hung above an old chest-of-drawers, I saw that I was smiling. I carefully put down the cardboard suitcase on an oriental carpet that had faded where the sun had faithfully shone for years on the same expanse of pattern, and I inhaled the smell of the house. Instinctively

145

I looked round for the apples that must be lying somewhere on the top of a cupboard, already set out in orderly rows; for the smoke of a forgotten cigarette, left to burn itself out in an ash-tray. A scent hovered in the air, as if the billowing of a woman's dress had scattered it like dew before leaving the house.

" Mademoiselle? "

A round-faced woman, armoured in an apron that covered her from shoulders to ankles, came up to me.

" Are you Sibylle's nurse? "

" Good afternoon, madame. Yes, I'm the nurse. . . ."

I did not utter Sibylle's name; I did not want to mention her; I was afraid of breaking the spell too soon.

" I'm the cook. . . . I'll come and show you your room," she said, holding out her hand.

Our hands had found an unexpected kinship in their rough contact. The first floor displayed great doors that gave on to the carpeted passage; the second of them presented me with " the surprise."

The cook showed me into a charming room with pink curtains and a pink counterpane; on a table, there was an ink-pot and some writing-paper. In this house I would write often to my parents.

The cook leant back against the wall.

" Is there anything you need? The bathroom on this floor is next to Sibylle's bedroom, the third door on the right as you come out. . . . I'm going downstairs now. I must get dinner ready."

I put my astonished suitcase down on a chair.

" Madame and the children, when will they be back? "

She gave a broad kindly smile.

" Madame went off with Monsieur and the children directly after breakfast. They'll be back just in time for dinner. Madame told me you'd be coming to-day. . . . Wouldn't you like something to eat? Have you had tea? "

" I'd very much like a glass of milk."

The big light kitchen had two windows open on the garden. The cook put a slice of bread and butter and a glass of milk in front of me on the table and sat down opposite me.

" My name's Rose; you can call me Rose. . . . And what's your name, mademoiselle? "

" Christine."

" Fancy, I've got a niece called Christine but she hasn't got fair hair. You, you're fair like Sibylle. Shall I cut you another slice? "

I was no longer in the least hungry, but I hoped she would tell me some more about this little girl, so I accepted.

" I think there are four children here, aren't there? And that the youngest is six."

She folded her hands on the table and explained to me:

" Sibylle's only five and a half. . . . She's as pretty as a picture."

I ventured on to more dangerous territory.

147

" Is she good? "

" Good? She's an angel. . . . I've told Madame ever so often that Sibylle didn't need a nurse. . . ."

With those words she had cruelly threatened my situation and my work. I put on a serious expression as if I had just arrived from a Swiss college with a highly-trained nurse's diploma.

" You know, a child always needs so much special care. And, besides, there are her brother and sisters. . . ."

" Four," replied Rose, as proudly as if she were their grandmother. " Two boys and two girls. But you'll only have Sibylle. . . ."

Suddenly she broke off and I felt I could see what she was thinking behind her shiny wrinkled forehead.

" What country do you come from? "

" From Hungaria."

The word Hungaria broke against the tiled walls and splintered in a thousand pieces on the floor. I was overwhelmed with an immense sadness; I clenched my teeth and fought desperately against my tears. Then, humiliated by their wet warmth, I let my head fall forward on the table.

" There, there, I didn't mean to make you cry— forgive me, mademoiselle. . . ."

How could I explain to her that I was not annoyed, that the word Hungary had opened the floodgates? All those secret sorrows I had repressed had revolted. I was crying for the life I had dreamed of; I missed my parents; Georges was far away. And galled by weariness and by·the eternal question: " What country do you come from? " I would have liked to relapse into being a child again. Independence and loneliness were too hard.

I felt her heavy hand on my hair; I raised my head; she was crying too. She pulled her chair up close to mine.

" It won't go on for ever."

I searched for my handkerchief.

" I don't want to go back there but I *would* like a home."

With her clean starched apron and her white hair, she was like an old nurse for whom life and death no longer hold any secrets. If I could lay my head on that shoulder, how gladly I would recover the past— peace, the country, childhood!

She said, almost in my ear:

" You just see how happy you're going to be here. Madame's so nice and the children aren't naughty like other children."

I wanted to protest that there were no naughty children but I was too exhausted to defend anything whatever.

I went up to my room again; I closed the door behind me, and sat down on my narrow bed. With a tired gesture I pulled off the coverlet and let myself drop, with my eyes closed and my head against the pillow.

The noise of a car made me start. Staggering from this brief violent sleep, I went over to the wash-basin and washed my face in cold water. When I went down the hall was already full of people. I looked for a landmark and found it in Madame's face. I had seen her once in the office of the organisation which had recommended me but only for a few minutes. Here, she advanced towards me, her face radiant. . . .

" Good evening, Christine. . . . Have you been here long? "

" I arrived about four."

The children were clinging round her in a little crowd; she introduced them one by one.

" This is Sibylle. . . ."

The little girl, with her big periwinkle-blue eyes, held out her hand.

" Say how do you do," insisted Madame.

I could hardly hear the faint voice.

" How do you do? . . ."

Madame added:

" Christine."

And Sibylle repeated: " Christine."

Madame went on:

" And these are Bruno, Gabriel, Odette and Mireille."

All those young faces were turned towards me. Their grave thoughtful looks scrutinised me. Madame hastily banished this tiny awkward silence.

" Children, this is Christine. I've told you quite enough about her for you to welcome her as nicely as possible. So make an effort to be a little more agreeable than usual."

The front door opened.  It was Monsieur.

" Ah! " he said.  " You're here.  Good evening, mademoiselle;  did you have a good journey? "

After a few minutes' chatting, Madame came upstairs with me and the children to show me their rooms and explain my work.

" You'll have nothing to do for Gabriel, Odette and Mireille.  You'll look after Sibylle and, very occasionally, Bruno. . . .  But we're late to-night;  the children must have their baths."

That evening passed in a pleasant whirl.  I soaped Sibylle's frail body energetically;  she had not yet asked me where I came from.  She was submissive and I was suspicious.  This goodness put me on my guard.  Bruno was playing submarines in the bath and did not want to come out of the water.

At last, at eight o'clock, we were all sitting round the big table in the dining-room.  I sat beside Sibylle and kept an eye on her to see that she ate enough.  As I came in, I had seen a picture but, at the moment, it was behind me and it intrigued me greatly.  I had been struck by its sober beauty and its muted light. Rose waited on us;  I was embarrassed when she offered me the dish;  I had cried on her shoulder and I ought not to let her wait on me.  But she found this perfectly natural.

Madame had very beautiful hair with long plaits wound round her head like a crown.  Monsieur had admiring glances for his wife, an absent-minded smile for us and a diet for himself.

The pleasantly slow rhythm of that dinner, the children's subdued chatter, the warm light of the table, the garden wrapped in the semi-darkness of that mild evening and the presence of that extraordinary picture I had noticed on entering the room, enhanced the personality of Madame. She kept the conversation going effortlessly; she had a word for each child, as if distributing sweets with scrupulous fairness; she made an intimate gesture towards her husband, laying her hand on his and, for a moment, they exchanged looks; she inquired after Rose's health and talked about a woman friend she had visited in the afternoon. Her regular, intelligent beauty was neither eclipsed nor emphasised by her crown of hair; she was one of those rare women who can carry the weight of long hair without being vinegarish or bad-tempered. She had a clear forehead. Her light grey eyes, with a speck of green in the iris, rested now and then on the silver dish of fruit that stood in the middle of the table. In those fleeting moments of absence, she was dreamy, almost defenceless, intimately engaged in some thought that was exclusively her own. But the voices of the children instantly brought her back to reality, and she returned to the conversation, sure of herself and of her secret.

When we left the table I found myself at last face to face with the picture. It represented a grave man with his profile shadowed by a large hat.

I ventured a supposition:

" School of Rembrandt? "

" It is a Rembrandt," answered Monsieur, in a pleasant unemotional voice.

I took Sibylle by the hand, and, as I walked towards the staircase, I felt happy for the first time for a very long while.

" Christine. . . ."

Madame's voice made me turn my head towards her; we stopped with the child on one of the stairs.

" Yes, madame."

" I'm so sorry but I must tell you I've had a letter from the nurse who's been with us for four years. She had to go off to Holland because her mother was ill. And, in to-day's letter, she writes that she will get one of her sisters to look after her mother so that she can come back to us. So I can't keep you longer than a month. But don't worry, my husband and I between us will find you something else. You do understand, don't you? "

" But, of course, I understand, madame."

She raised her head and smiled at me.

" Don't be frightened, we'll arrange it all."

I went on climbing the stairs with Sibylle. Her little hand became warm and friendly in my own. She spoke to me for the first time.

" It's a pity you've got to go. The other nurse is nice, but perhaps you can stay all the same. . . ."

In her little room, I took off her dressing-gown and put her to bed.

" Will you tell me a story? Bring one of my books, they're on the bookshelf."

153

I told her a long story, and, after having tucked her well into her blankets, I went to my room.

The writing-paper on the table had become useless. This month would go so fast. But what should I do afterwards?

The next day, when I took Sibylle and Bruno in to Madame, I saw that she was writing on a typewriter.

" I translate books," she explained to me.

Almost instinctively I said to the children:

" Come along with me; your mother mustn't be disturbed."

She gave me a look of astonishment.

" That's certainly the first time I've heard those words in this house! "

Seeing her typewriter, the papers scattered over the table, a pencil fallen on the carpet—all this in the shafts of autumn sunlight—gave me an irresistible longing to tell her that I imagined a life exactly like hers, with a work in hand and children coming in to greet me in the morning. But I virtuously kept silence and took Sibylle off for a walk.

It was an unforgettable month, saturated with joys and sorrows. I counted the days like a prisoner voluntarily locked up in her bliss of provisional peace. I wrote optimistic letters to my parents and I saw Georges every Sunday. He had found a chauffeur's job with one of those numerous White Russian princes who had survived the 1917 revolution. This prince lived alone in Paris in a sumptuous flat, looked after by a faithful cook. Georges who, in Hungary, had been given a little car as a birthday present by his parents, had had no qualms about accepting the job which made him the driver of an enormous luxury car, black and shining as an undertaker's in a funeral procession. It was a very famous car, of the kind built to order for millionaires, and on account of the classic shape of its body, no one suspected that it dated from 1927. From information supplied by the cook, Georges learnt that, long ago, the jovial prince with his blotchy, perpetually smiling face had married an immensely rich American and that they lived apart; she in America, with her title of Princess, and he with the money she sent him every month.

Our Sundays were filled with the stories we exchanged about the charms of Sibylle and the caprices of the prince. Georges drove him nearly every night to a night-club near Pigalle and he studied his International Law by the light of the little lamp in the car. But this car deliberately stalled its engine at the moment the red light changed to green. Georges was harassed by impatient klaxons that suddenly hooted all round them and the prince would pull down the window that separated them so that the latter would be sure of hearing his oaths. " We must have a life of our own . . ." We were always repeating those magic words.

At the end of the third week, Madame sent me to see a family in their neighbourhood; she believed they were looking for a nurse for their child. I was invited in and carefully examined. My physical strength did not appear adequate to the work required. " You are frail and the house is large," they told me.

Madame was extremely upset; she would have liked to keep two nurses rather than send me out into a blank future. They never spoke of my lost country nor of my life as a refugee. They listened to everything I said in my strongly accented French; we talked about Balzac and Roger Martin du Gard. They were surprised that we had so much knowledge of French literature in Hungary but this surprise was never expressed; I was only aware of it in their eyes. During my long walks with Sibylle I learnt the French I had not known before, the language of everyday life and children's favourite expressions. Sibylle corrected me with gay confidence. Once I asked her the question:

" Now, tell me, what *is* dreaming? "

She answered without hesitation:

" Thinking while you're asleep. . . ."

By making her define a word I had wanted to disarm her. I had hoped that I would be the one to explain it to her; I wanted to enjoy the cheap superiority of the grown-up who sets a problem with the certainty that the child cannot solve it. But this little fairy of five and a half got the better of me in intelligence and quickness of mind.

When I departed from Garches, leaving my provisional happiness for only too certain anxieties, Madame gave me an envelope with two months' wages in it instead of one. And her children, who had been born with white socks and had never had a grazed knee, kissed me, one by one, with that look typical of their age; a look full of curiosity, but passionless and detached. Sibylle said in a choked little voice:

" Will you come back to see me? "

" Yes, of course Christine will come back," replied Madame.

Rose had given me a box of sweets; she greatly regretted that I had not had a chance to meet her niece who was also called Christine.

It was Monsieur who drove me back to Paris. He deposited me outside the little hotel.

" Au revoir, mademoiselle."

" Au revoir, monsieur."

Perhaps some day, I *shall* see them again?

# 12

WITH MY two months' wages in my handbag, I decided to hire a typewriter and launch out on my great adventure—writing my first novel: *Wanda*. Now that I was back in Paris, Georges often dropped in to see me, and the little street was overcome by the sight of such a sumptuous car. But one day the engine stalled right in front of the door and Georges, surrounded by a mocking crowd, could not manage to start it up again.

The prince had worries; the money from America was in arrears and it was the cook who paid Georges. It was she who lent her master money so that he should not miss his evening's entertainment.

The little table in my room barely supported the weight of the huge typewriter. It was a double-bank Remington. The rickety keyboard groaned when I touched the keys, and, at the end of each line, the bell rang so violently that my neighbour, an English-woman, asked me several times to change my machine. I had to explain that this was impossible. I wrote in the midst of these shrill noises. I cooked on a board laid over the wash-basin and the spirit-stove puffed and snorted like the first steam engine.

How does one write a novel? I had my characters, the quickening pace of an action whose end I could not foresee, the face of a woman and the atmosphere of Vienna. I paced up and down the tiny room and, one morning, I found my opening sentence: *The soldier brutally grabbed hold of Wanda* ... I did not yet know which of the soldiers—I foresaw five of them—made this rough, decisive gesture, but, with those words, I was launched on my first chapter. I typed for seven or eight hours a day and, when I went out during the afternoon, I had an intoxicated sense of well-being and marvellous calm for which my own pages were responsible.

The weather changed and the rain imprisoned me in the little hotel bedroom. Georges came whenever he could get a free moment and we talked about our future. He explained to me that success was only a question of luck, backed up by an ingenious idea. It was about this time that he put an advertisement in an evening paper, whose text ran as follows: "Young man requires capital of one million (possibly more) to launch publicity campaign for sensational invention. Immense profit for lender. I will negotiate loan in 24 hours. Address reply to this paper, Urgent."

He would like me to have been more optimistic but, when he told me the principles of his invention, his enthusiasm filled me with alarm. He wanted to manufacture a refrigerator without ice. His plans were astounding and, in the end, he decided to set up the apparatus, piece by piece, in my room.

" But how will you get the electric current? " I asked timidly.

He was knocked off his perch and almost hostile when I recalled him to the brute facts of hotel life. I had wanted to change the bulb of my lamp for a stronger one and we had had a short-circuit. The proprietor was determined to keep his expenses down.

He went off in a bad temper, and, alone once more, I went over our conversation. It was only after he had gone that I realised the implication of certain words. " There's only two years difference between us. When you're thirty, I shall be a man of thirty-two. Just imagine the difference. A man of thirty is only beginning his life, whereas a woman . . ." His silence had been eloquent. Nowadays I understood his silences better than his words.

That evening, my eyes were too tired to write. Under cover of darkness, hiding behind my burning eyelids, I thought I had still nine years of youth left.

Monsieur Szabo appeared in our life like a shooting star promising the fulfilment of every secret hope. His name seemed to destine him to be a Hungarian like any other Hungarian, but he was totally different from any I had met hitherto. His round head, with its friendly, shining baldness, and his generous gestures—he would give a five hundred franc tip after drinking a fifty franc coffee—had made his reputation in an elegant tea-shop not far from the Champs-Elysées. We knew that he had been a big business man in Hungary; before the war, according to the respectful gossips who hovered round him, he had sold wheat by the truck-load and sheep by the flock. He lived in a luxurious villa just outside Paris and never went anywhere without an old Pole who acted both as his chauffeur and as his indispensable interpreter. Monsieur Szabo did not know a single word of French and said his friendly " good morning " to the smiling waitresses in Hungarian. He had left Hungary in the last days of the war and had apparently succeeded in getting an entire train full of merchandise through defeated Germany. Switzerland had accepted Monsieur Szabo and his train and, a few years later, he had arrived in Paris with the remains of his fortune and a severe Swiss wife who had given him four children in five years.

The red nape of his neck mounted guard over two small ears which nature had carefully stuck flat against his skull and his quick eyes darted from objects to people and rested on both with the same interest.

Georges was the first to have the idea to ask Monsieur Szabo to lend him some capital. But it was no longer a question of the refrigerator; we wanted to have the management of a little restaurant and to make a fortune thanks to homely, wholesome cooking.

I would have preferred to remain in my little room and go on writing, without thinking of the world about me, but the sum I possessed when I left Garches was diminishing very fast and I looked every day at the advertisements to find another place as nurse. Moreover, Georges wanted to leave the prince and the car in which he had to keep vigil every night outside the famous Pigalle night-club. Through an agency we had discovered a *bistro* whose present manageress wished to leave. The agent had explained to us that the restaurant was in a working-class district and that, on account of its situation, its future was assured with a minimum of work.

"I shall serve in the bar and you'll do the cooking," Georges told me, his eyes shining with enthusiasm. "I shall work till dawn but you'll go to bed as soon as possible because you'll buy the provisions in the big market, the Halles, and you'll have to get up very early."

Monsieur Szabo listened to our projects with the faintly absent-minded attention of big business men who have to solve several problems at once. The Pole never left his side and, barricaded behind a trolley loaded with cakes which the waitress left constantly within his reach, he put questions to us. After long complicated conversations it was agreed that he should give us the sum necessary to start us off and that, for several years, he should have a percentage of the receipts.

He looked at me very uneasily.

"Do you know how to cook for forty or fifty people?"

I assured him that I did but I was paralysed with terror.

It was also necessary to envisage a Frenchman who would act as a dummy and take the restaurant in his name. As refugees we could not get the necessary permits.

One day we were invited to Monsieur Szabo's home and we made the acquaintance of his wife. She was a tall, bony blonde with cold eyes and fat hips. She openly despised us and the languishing conversation in bad German made me sleepy and frightened. During luncheon I felt Madame Szabo's sharp gaze hovering over my head, brushing my hair and settling on my plate like an obstinate wasp that refuses to go away before it has stung you.

" Are your children well, madame? "

" Very, very well," she answered, and she rolled her " r's " so strongly that I suddenly imagined those noisy " r's " were roller-skates that she attached to her tongue every time she spoke.

" They're at Basle, with my mother, for a fortnight. . . ."

Monsieur Szabo helped himself to another large slice of meat that had already gone cold in its sauce, for the servant had forgotten to remove the dish and left it on the table.

Madame Szabo exclaimed:

" Your stomach! . . . Don't make yourself ill— think of your children! . . ."

She went on, with a violence unusual in big blonde women:

" You must be careful about that restaurant too. Losing money's a great deal easier than making it. Think of your children's future. . . ."

Her husband shrugged his shoulders, unmoved, and wiped his plate with a piece of bread.

" Don't be afraid, Hilda; it's not a bad enterprise and they've got courage. Besides, think of the three thousand typewriters I'm waiting for."

Up till now, taking refuge in a feigned indifference, I had let the words go on swirling round me. I was as morally weary as I was physically and the presence of Georges now seemed an enigma rather than a solution. Did he really believe that I should be able to cope with that amount of work? He had promised me a little maid to do the washing-up and, later on, a waitress. He had so much confidence in my strength and thought I was so courageous that I had not dared to disillusion him. I wanted to be the woman of his dreams. The word " typewriter " came as a pleasant surprise. Suddenly awakened I turned to Monsieur Szabo:

" Are you talking about typewriters? "

I looked at his lips, all shiny with grease and at an audacious little drop that was making its way towards his chin.

" I'm waiting for three thousand typewriters from the United States. I shall break the European market with this influx of cheap machines. After that, I shall order them by tens of thousands."

" Could I buy one? I'd so much like to. . . ."

His broad smile made the drop run down on to his neck; I no longer saw it.

" Nothing easier," he replied. " You can have two if you like. . . ."

The maid brought in some fruit. Madame Szabo attacked an apple and Monsieur Szabo took a banana.

Georges shot a question across the table like a bullet.

" Shall we go and see the restaurant to-morrow? "

" About three o'clock? . . ." said Monsieur Szabo reflectively.

I broke in, excited by the thought of my future typewriter:

" It would be better to go in the evening. During the rush hours the agent says there are lots of people. . . ."

He agreed.

" Come and fetch me at the tea-shop at six; we'll all go together in the car."

Madame Szabo once more addressed her husband as if we were not present.

" Have you really got confidence in them? "

" Why, of course I have. They're fine, courageous young things. . . ."

" But it's our money that's in question," she insisted. " The children . . ."

Oh, those children! I saw them as famished monsters who drank a glass of liquid silver for breakfast and ate bundles of crisp thousand-franc notes instead of rolls.

We left the overheated villa about four in the afternoon. The cold wind slipped under the collar of my old winter coat and ran all down my back. I carefully avoided the puddles for my shoes were no longer good for anything but dry, sunny weather. I

166

shivered, and Georges, who was holding my arm, asked me:

" Is there anything wrong? Why are you depressed? "

His boyish face was full of frank curiosity. He was not laughing at me. He really wanted to know. But how could I explain our own situation to him? I loathed his man's hat, that hat that made him look so absurdly young. All the same he was twenty-three, nearly twenty-four. . . .

I did not answer till we were in the métro and the kindly underground warmth enveloped me.

" There's nothing the matter with me, absolutely nothing."

He said, in a business-like way:

" You mustn't be ill, now that we're going to have our *bistro*."

Without comment I silently fixed my eyes on the black walls of those extraordinary tunnels along which the métro was running at full speed. He took my motionless hand in his. Did we love each other? . . .

From the very first moment I had felt a profound antipathy towards Monsieur Szabo's interpreter and he reciprocated my hostility without disguising his feelings. He had the head of a worn-out old *roué* on a thin, wrinkled neck and his almost skeleton-like hand was always nervously brushing the revers of his coat that shone like the seat of an old pair of trousers. Leaning on his stick, with his hat laid on the table beside his empty cup, he would watch us like a bird of prey whose age has dimmed its keen sight so that it has to stoop lower and lower in order not to miss its victim. He spoke French and Hungarian well enough to translate Monsieur Szabo's sentences and, in our presence, he rushed the words out quicker than ever so as to show off his prowess as an interpreter.

Before we left the tea-shop Monsieur Szabo dismissed him with a " We'll meet later on, at the club," and, installed in our friend's car, we set off for the restaurant. Monsieur Szabo drove very badly, making his brakes screech at the red lights that lit up along our route, bright and burning as little braziers that could resist that icy rain.

" Got stage fright? " asked Georges under his breath, and I had the feeling that, with that question whispered in the hollow of my ear, he was laying the whole burden of the enterprise on me.

" Yes, I have got stage fright," I answered aggressively like someone owning up to their fear with pride.

After minute researches on a very worn map, we found ourselves in a long and narrow street in Levallois. Monsieur Szabo advanced cautiously; an enormous lorry parked in the middle of the street blocked the view. Dark shapes, dripping with rain, were unloading the lorry, and by the light of the yellow street-lamps we saw split carcasses of bleeding beef on their broad shoulders.

The butcher was standing in the doorway of his shop observing these blood-stained shadows going to and fro and, when he saw Monsieur Szabo lower the car window and lean out as a sign of protest against the obstruction, he shouted some unknown words at him.

" What's he saying? " asked Monsieur Szabo, turning round to Georges.  Georges hastily replied:

" Oh, nothing important, he just wants you to go on being patient. . . ."

But this was untrue.  Behind Monsieur Szabo's back I gave Georges an inquiring look but he put his finger to his lips.

At last we were able to proceed and to search for the number.  I tried to catch sight of the restaurant through a misted pane.  Just when Monsieur Szabo was about to lose patience, we at last found our *bistro*.  From the street all we could see was a glass door with a check curtain and windows covered with the same stuff.  By a miracle a van was just moving off and Monsieur Szabo occupied its place.

Monsieur Szabo went in first and we followed him, submissive and trembling.  The restaurant was empty and, in the dimness of the back room, we could see chairs piled up on tables.  The front part was dominated by a zinc bar-counter and a kind of dresser with shelves.  Standing fixed and motionless in the bright light of the bar itself, we felt as if we were imprisoned in a luminous circle drawn by a magician.

And suddenly there appeared out of a dark corner a woman of overwhelming beauty, the kind of beauty blondes call common and men respect out of prudence.  Her masses of black hair, whose glossy curls shone

169

with brilliantine, and her plump, voluptuous, friendly shoulders, created expressly for men to lay their heads on that marvellous cushion of living flesh, presented a startling spectacle to us and intoxicating one to Monsieur Szabo.

" You've come about the business? "

Her voice invested the prosaic question with something intimate, almost sensual.

Monsieur Szabo turned to me excited and enchanted:

" What does she say? "

The young woman came towards us and I saw the shape of her long thighs under the tight sheath of her skirt.

Monsieur Szabo forgot that the restaurant was empty. He installed himself at the bar and the woman poured him out a drink. I watched in silence and we learnt that she was Spanish, that she had run the restaurant for the last two years but, because of a serious quarrel with her husband, she wanted to go back to Barcelona.

Georges faithfully translated her precious words and Monsieur Szabo, lulled by strong drink, leant on the counter and never took his dazed, admiring eyes off the voluptuous proprietress. She was not in the least embarrassed by the fact that the restaurant was empty.

" I haven't bothered about it since my trouble," she said, and her pointed breasts asserted themselves with shameless candour through her yellow jumper.

With a mechanical gesture she wiped some dry glasses; when she shook her head she set the big rings in her ears dancing.

I saw a juke-box in a corner. I slipped a coin into the slit indicated by an arrow; I wanted to furnish this emptiness. Georges was standing close by me, alert and expectant.

" Are you coming? " he said. " The woman speaks a little German and I've left Szabo with her. Now we can look over the restaurant. . . . Do you think Szabo will fork out? "

My answer was drowned in a burst of music and the waltz set everything spinning round me; the dust, the shadows, my own misery. It was too much for me: the " Blue Danube " fixed on a scratched record; the curtains whose folds were solid with encrusted dirt; the tables heaped with chairs; Monsieur Szabo and his swimming eyes, avid with the hope of possessing that body, at least in his dreams; the smell of stale beer and the thick cloaks of dust on the bottles.

" Oh, *do* come along," Georges insisted.

I went to see the sinister kitchen with its enormous saucepans suspended over a coal range.

" It's a bit old," Georges admitted. " But we'll get it all into condition again."

Through an open trap-door we descended into the cellar which was lit by one small electric bulb. The smell of mildew took us by the throat and enormous spider's webs were draped, motionless, over a cask that had entirely rotted away.

"You know what we'll do here, darling," said Georges. "We'll make a bar ... A frightfully smart bar. ... The French love cellars provided they're romantic or unusual. We'll repaint the walls and then we'll put up some artificial spider's webs. .... Maybe we might hang up a skeleton, cleverly lighted, in a corner. ... And, to please you, we'll stress the intellectual character of this bar ... it'll be a literary night-club. ... Later on, of course, we'll have an orchestra. D'you agree, darling?"

I preserved a hostile silence and I was afraid even to smile. When we went upstairs again we found Monsieur Szabo completely tipsy.

"I'll give you the money for the business," he mumbled thickly. "Even more than you wanted. .... Wonderful thing, youth. ...."

The Spanish woman smiled and planted her black gaze on us. She yawned behind the bar and, as she stretched her arms, the tight jumper nearly split over her breasts.

"How glad I shall be to be back in Barcelona," she sighed.

This did not surprise me. I, too, would much rather be in Barcelona than here.

When we left Monsieur Szabo outside his club he thanked us, almost with tears in his eyes, for our excursion. He also promised us the money we needed to sign the contract at the beginning of the following week. We accompanied him right to the door of the elegant building.

When he was in the lift Georges asked the porter:
" What's his club, that gentleman who's just gone upstairs? "

The porter replied with great disdain:

" It's a gaming club: baccarat and roulette. . . . But exclusively for members."

I hastily stifled a wicked hope. " If he lost his money, there'd be no more restaurant! . . ." I did not dare say a word. Georges was too worried.

After that we only saw Monsieur Szabo in the waiting-room of his club. He promised us the money from one day to the next and it was always about six o'clock that we arrived in this richly furnished little drawing-room which, for us, was furnished only with anxiety. I took not the slightest notice of another woman who was waiting for some man and I put my sopping shoes against the radiator.

A helpless, frantic Georges asked me the same question every time:

" Do you think he'll sign the cheque to-day? "

I shrugged my shoulders, disguising my lassitude as much as I could and, huddled in a soft, well-upholstered arm-chair, I said nothing.

When he arrived we stood motionless, almost hypnotised in his presence. Every day he would burst into the room with his hands outstretched, always with the same overwhelming enthusiasm.

" My dear young friends, how ashamed I am to keep you waiting like this, but I couldn't leave the table."

His congested face, his eyes with their network of red veins, the thick finger he thrust between his collar and his swollen neck to assist his breathing, the overnight beard flourishing on his chin like the bluish imprint of some strange malady, inspired us with a kind of terror.

"The estate agent has given us just one week more," Georges would explain and in the heavily furnished, never-aired room his voice sounded abnormally loud.

"But, with a week, we've got all eternity before us," Monsieur Szabo would say joyfully, and he would add:

"I've got to get my luck back. My interpreter wins all the time, playing with *my* money; it doesn't make sense. . . ."

Already his gaze was turning towards the door.

"I must go back, dear children."

One day, I intercepted that look and, staring at the contracted pupils, I searched for the light of reason, for the proof that he was still capable of sustained thought.

"Monsieur Szabo," I said. "Why don't you go back to the tea-shop? All your business is waiting there for you to attend to it. . . . And the typewriters. . . . What's happened to them?"

He bit his lower lip and its thick flesh retained the sharp imprint of the tooth.

"They're in the customs at the moment, I can't pay the duty."

I insisted cruelly, feeling as if I were hitting an unconscious man:

" And your children, Monsieur Szabo—are they all right? "

Tiny drops of sweat beaded his dilated pores.  It was as if a strange dew had covered his face.

" I've sent my wife to her parents in Switzerland.  The villa was too expensive but she'll come back as soon as I've bought a flat."

The woman, who was listening to our conversation, lowered her heavy eyelids, as if she were hearing that phrase for the hundredth time.  Suddenly, the unknown woman became an ally; I wanted to turn to her and say, in the most natural way:

" Are you waiting for a madman too, dear? "

The door opened and we saw two men standing there; the interpreter and a thin little man who rushed up to the woman mumbling:

" Everything's going splendidly, love."

" Come home with me," said the woman in a dull, unimpassioned voice.

The thin little man was overflowing with jovial good humour. . . .

" You go, love, and I'll be back soon."

The woman raised clear eyes, shining with hatred, then she whispered with an impassiveness that made our flesh creep:

" Moron. . . ."

The little man came up very close to her and whispered something with his lips pressed against her ear.

The interpreter, still standing in the open doorway, shot a word of command at Monsieur Szabo.

" Hi, come back, you! "

" Is that how he speaks to you now? "

The remark came out entirely against my will.

Monsieur Szabo, already on his feet, held out his moist hand to us.

" He's a friend, a good old intimate friend. . . . And he understands gambling. It was he who introduced me here. . . ."

To show his impatience, the Pole drummed on the door:

" Hurry up, old chap. . . ."

He was animated by the excitement of his all too easy revenge. He took Monsieur Szabo by the arm, like an attendant in a lunatic asylum conducting his patient back into the insane ward after a visit from the outside world.

In the cold, harsh street, Georges turned to me.

" Do you think he's going to stop gambling? If he doesn't, he's a lost man. But, after all, that's how it always is in life. . . . Once a drunkard, always a drunkard. . . ."

A hitherto unknown rebelliousness made me bristle up at these bromides. I shook myself like a dog trying to get rid of its collar.

" How on earth should I know? What we've got to do during the next five days is find a job."

" We might have been so happy with the *bistro*,"

Georges went on, without even noticing my despairing fury.

It was one of his greatest qualities, this ability to dream. He went on his way in life with the terrifying serenity of a sleepwalker who walks over the roofs, unconsciously reassured because the people around him are awake and have sufficient tact not to waken him abruptly. . . .

I no longer understood anything about him. What had I to do with his body there beside my own and with his grey thoughts? I wrote enthusiastic letters to my parents; I was so used to my own lies about a pleasant life, full of work, but lit up with all sorts of possibilities that, when I had finished a letter, I was almost happy. I lulled myself with my own words and I kept on telling myself that it was marvellous to be in Paris, to be twenty-two and to have a great romantic love. But the truth was far otherwise. The meaning of my life, adorned by the elements I would have liked to believe genuine, was hidden in the pages of my novel. I knew already that I was born to write but I felt too, that, before my work was published, I ought to keep quiet about it. To be published! . . . I looked at the names of publishers in the windows of bookshops and I sometimes went inside without any possibility of being able to buy anything. I would shyly ask for some information and I would savour the smell of books and touch their covers. I had done a hundred pages of *Wanda*; she had achieved her third lover and, when I was very hungry while working, I stuffed her with foie gras and champagne. I wrote with blankets wrapped round my thighs and my old coat over my shoulders, but *she* was spoilt and her flat in Vienna was so warmly heated that she walked about barefoot on the thick carpets. At one time when I lay listless and depressed in Georges's arms, I had just made her swoon with pleasure at the end of a chapter. I envied Wanda. . . .

# 13

MADAME SAULNER, our new employer, was tall, without being fat.  She liked wholesome cooking, finished her meal with yoghourt, wore a well-disciplined smile on her face and starched collars round her neck.  Her domestic world was made to her measure.  A huge twelve-roomed flat; eight tall children of whom the six boys had their mother's round eyes; a kitchen perfectly equipped to deal with all these ferocious appetites.  The table in the dining-room always presented the same problem when I had to clean it.  Covered with a plastic cloth, this table was as big as a skating-rink; I had to climb on a chair to wipe away the wine stains in the middle of it.  The children might drink a glass of wine at each meal.  It seemed it was good for their health whereas we, in the kitchen, were condemned to the water tap.  Madame was very thrifty but she also had a highly developed sense of responsibility.  She did not want to expose her staff to the temptation of becoming drunkards.

When we came to this luxury flat for the first time, in reply to a small advertisement, the concierge pounced out of her lodge; she was a cantankerous woman whose black frock, obviously given her by one of her tenants, lent her a sham air of distinction.  She asked us suspiciously:

"Where are you going?"

"To see Madame Saulner. ...."

Her look became evasive and she repeated, with avid curiosity:

"You're going to see Madame Saulner? ...  Is it about the advertisement or a personal call?"

"The advertisement. ...."

Victorious, she indicated the back stairs, which ran straight up from the street, on the left of the main entrance.

So, very suitably, we arrived in Madame Saulner's flat by way of the kitchen.  The cook showed us into the drawing-room.

"What do you think of her?" Georges asked me. He wanted to know my opinion before having one of his own.

I could not answer because Madame Saulner had just come in.  Shaking hands with us so forcefully that she crushed my wedding-ring painfully into my finger, she said:

"I engage you; your references are good."

The cook brought in a tray with three cups, a tin of powdered coffee and a jug of hot water.

Madame Saulner poured us out some coffee, and, with a brusque gesture, held out the sugar bowl to me.

"Sugar?  How much?"

It was as if she had said: "Arsenic?  How much?"

She added, gazing at me:

" Are you an intellectual too? "

That little " too " was like a slap in the face, but I had no shoes and I wanted to keep my hired typewriter. I answered meekly:

" I don't know, madame."

" Because *you*," she went on, turning to Georges, " you wanted to go on studying, didn't you? "

Georges was astonishingly firm.

" I *am* going on studying, madame."

She shivered and a little grimace turned down the corners of her smile.

" I don't know if that will do here; there's a great deal of work. . . ."

Georges replied obstinately:

" I shall find a little time, madame."

She gave a short nervous laugh.

" You know your own mind. . . ."

She came back to me, like a dog with two bones who gnaws first one, then the other:

" When did you leave your own country? "

" In 1948, madame."

" Your studies? "

" I took my School Leaving Certificate and University Entrance. I did eight years Latin at school."

" Ah, did you indeed? Well, well . . ."

She was so surprised that she stopped chewing her bone for a moment or two.

" You could help my elder daughter, Patricia; she's not very keen on Latin. . . ."

Instinctively compelled into a duel that amused me, I told her:

" I also did six years at the Conservatoire. I nearly became a pianist. . . ."

Madame Saulner fell into a dangerous torpor; she repeated under her breath:

" Conservatoire . . . Patricia plays the piano too. You could take her teacher's place."

Georges, who had not the faintest notion that an extraordinary battle had just begun, put in, with innocent candour:

" Christine is writing a book. She has a great deal of talent."

The match was already very near the gunpowder. Madame Saulner exclaimed:

" I want a housemaid . . . a good housemaid! On Sunday afternoons, you can do whatever you like, even write. But during the week, I warn you, I will not stand for any deviation from your work. . . . Do you darn well, Christine? "

I did not like hearing my name on her lips. I would like to have invented another name and proffered it to her on my palm, as one shows a coin one has found behind a cupboard. I should like to have said I was called Catherine or Rose—why not Antigone?

" Are you day-dreaming, Christine? "

It was her declaration of war: " Are you day-dreaming, Christine? "

We spent the month of November like shipwrecked

people keeping their heads above the waves while they wait for a ship. But there was neither ship nor lifeboat for us. There was only Madame Saulner and her voice; her voice that galloped in front of her like a messenger; her voice that made me tremble; her sugary voice that was so sure of itself.

"What are you doing, Christine? Are you day-dreaming?"

Georges had a green apron and I had a white apron. Hélène, the cook, never stirred out of her kitchen. It was Madame Saulner who did the shopping; she did not wish Hélène to grow rich too quickly in her service. We were up at seven and we went to bed at eleven after having washed up a mountain of dirty crockery. Georges was as pale as a ghost and I had no idea how I looked myself: I avoided looking-glasses. The kind Hélène, who had already lost some years off her life in Madame's service, was a philosopher. She helped me as much as she could and supported me physically and morally; her affection was inexhaustible. She had no husband and no private life; her destiny was to be a slave but she had a marvellously warm heart. How should I ever have stood up to that life without her?

Georges pressed Monsieur's innumerable pairs of trousers. Monsieur was extremely insignificant. It was only his trousers that made me aware of his presence. During meals, I waited at table. I often thought of a housemaid we used to have in Budapest. She never smiled. Was she as unhappy as I was?

Madame Saulner always kept me waiting when I presented the heavy tray to her.

She pretended not to know I was behind her; she hated me and felt the need to express her hatred whenever she had the chance. When she condescended to take the meat, she promptly put the dishes back on the tray.

" But it's cold. . . . You people in the kitchen, are you incapable of serving our food hot? "

I would return to the kitchen with the meat. Hélène, scarlet with indignation, would exclaim:

" But it was piping hot! "

And the business would begin all over again.

We began our luncheon when they rose from the table. Madame's impatient steps would echo along the passage and we would eat hurriedly, our muscles contracted.

One day she came raging into the kitchen:

" I find you waste a great deal of time over your meals. You take longer to eat than we do, the family! "

I did not want to look at her; I fixed my eyes on the rim of my plate, but I could feel my legs shaking. I braced my feet against the tiles; I wanted to stop shaking, but the trembling ran through my whole body and I, who had not prayed for a long time, said inwardly:

" Oh God, make her go away, make her disappear; oh, God, make her be less unkind. . . ."

Madame Saulner invented apparently delicate tasks

184

in order to entrust them to me. She had a real silk nightdress, pleated from neck to hem. She would wear it for one night and give it to me to iron the following morning. For a whole week I did this pointless ironing; she watched me with satisfaction out of the corner of her eye. During that period of ironing, I took certain notes for my novel *Wanda*, and I wrote key-sentences on scraps of paper. " Frigid women adore luxurious nightdresses. For them real silk is a kind of sexual satisfaction. Wanda's friend was as big and strong as a horse; at night, she wrapped her large body in fine lace and repelled her husband's advances with disgust."

But, as my bedroom had no key, I had to hide my manuscript every day in my suitcase and push it under my bed.

In their drawing-room there was a book-case. Wiping off the dust I looked at the titles. Henry Bordeaux was most in evidence, followed by Duvernois and Pierre Benoit. The Comtesse de Ségur took up an entire shelf; I could not bear her and I always left a layer of dust over the misfortunes of that perverse, detestable Sophie. I do not like this unconsummated marriage between the Russian soul and a French name. I had a keen desire to re-read Cholokhov, Gogol, and, above all, Tchehov, but I consoled myself with the thought that, even if my favourite books were presented to me on a silver platter, I would be unable to read them. At eleven o'clock at night, I fell into bed, dead with exhaustion.

Madame Saulner had a great weakness for Georges. She tried to chat with him to prove that she too had a mind that was no stranger to social problems. Georges's nerves were infinitely more robust than my own and, with impeccable politeness, he did chat, if Madame was so inclined.

For the winter holidays, we went off to their country house which Georges and I had to clean from top to bottom in one morning. Hélène told us that, every time they came here, they invited a young Englishman, because it was very smart to have an English boy for the holidays!

How happy Madame was in that country house! She was always running up and down the stairs; she was so sorry we were not seeing her house with its spring flowers and she assured us, like a threat, that we should often be coming back here. In Paris we did have our Sundays from three o'clock on. Here, the situation was hopeless; there was no village anywhere near and we were entirely delivered over to Madame. Nevertheless she did send us out for an hour's walk on Sundays. " Take advantage of the air, my friends; take good, deep breaths of it. . . ."

The Englishman arrived on the Monday. He was a youth of seventeen whose transparent skin was not ruined by adolescent pimples. He was tall, slim and fair-haired, and he did not speak a word of French. He reminded me of Dickens, of the unforgettable David Copperfield, and I offered him the tray at meals with the loving care of a faithful reader meeting her favourite hero at long last in the flesh. Out in the kitchen, from which I could see the garden, I followed him with my eyes, as I did the washing-up, and I thought of my uncle and aunt who always spoke English when they talked about literature and who quarrelled in Italian because my uncle had lived for many years in Fiume. Heavens, how far away they were! Not because they were dead, but because of the life I was living now.

Hélène laid her heavy hand on my shoulder:

" Something wrong, little one? "

" I'm so tired, Hélène."

" You're not cut out for this work," she said. " You'll ruin your health if you keep on at it. . . . Couldn't you find something else? "

I answered lethargically:

" I don't know. I don't know anything any more. . . ."

Two days later when I went into the English boy's bedroom I smelt a peculiar smell. I opened the window, I swept the room and made his bed, but the smell obstinately persisted. I thought it was only my imagination. However, the next morning, I was aware of the same smell, only stronger, more diffused; in fact, definitely established.

At first I summoned Hélène; she sniffed with me and said, shrugging her shoulders:

" Madame was very unpleasant to the builders when they were rebuilding the house. Perhaps they've hidden something in the brickwork, as a revenge. A dead mouse. . . ."

" Do you think a sweet little mouse could produce such a stench ? "

Hélène was not sure.

" I don't know, but a decaying corpse does stink, you know. . . ."

With much regret I had to take Madame into my confidence. She came while the young Englishman was out on an excursion organised by Monsieur.

She planted herself in the middle of the room, and, with quivering nostrils, tried to define the smell. Then, without a word to me, she literally flung herself on the English boy's possessions. She opened the wardrobe and emptied it in one sweep. She removed a suitcase from the top of a cupboard and, placing it at her feet, she opened it. With a shout of victory, she drew out a round box with a red label: a Camembert! We all laughed together, Madame, Hélène and myself. We laughed till the tears ran down our cheeks and, when we recovered our gravity, we had only to look at the box to burst out laughing again. Madame was almost likeable when she laughed. Perhaps I had been mistaken; perhaps I had been morbidly sensitive; in that wild, hysterical giggling I was ready to become her ally, to serve her smilingly, without resentment. That blessed laugh made it possible to envisage the beginning of a friendship. . . . But she recovered her breath and stammered out:

" Oh, all these foreigners. . . . It's fantastic, how stupid they are. . . ."

I turned to ice once more waiting for the allusion to my accent. My accent sometimes got on Madame's nerves. But she said not another word and went off with the cheese.

The next day, at luncheon, the English boy admitted that he had wanted to take a Camembert home to his family; he was completely bewildered by the general mirth.

I hardly ever had a chance to talk to Georges now. We were submerged under the work. He polished floors all day and the unleashed children ran all over the shining parquet with their snow-covered boots. Madame did not want me to darn the socks in the room where Georges was cleaning the silver.

" If you chatter you'll both work more slowly. Besides, you have the whole evening to yourselves. . . ."

Having said this, she vanished from the room.

Would she not, one day, also vanish from our lives?

# 14

AFTER THE winter holidays we returned to Paris.
There was also a Christmas Day whose memory I
want to blot out. I found my big typewriter covered
with dust; I went on paying its hire with desperate
tenacity and, whenever I could, I added a few words
to my manuscript.

It was on the day after our return, when I was
handing round the salad, that I was seized with an
attack of dizziness. The back of Madame's neck
became enormous, the table grew blurred and looked
like a great sheet of ice melting in the sun. I put down
the salad-bowl and ran into the scullery where I
collapsed in Hélène's arms.

" I'm ill, Hélène; I want to be sick. . . ."

She gave me a large glass of water and Georges
appeared too, looking astonished.

" Are you ill ? " he inquired incredulously.

" Go away," I said. " Get on with serving the
salad. I've left the salad-bowl in there."

I leant against the wicker back of the chair I was
sitting on; my legs had gone flabby and no longer
seemed to belong to me. I listened to the wild, irregular beating of my heart. It was the first time I

had seen Hélène's head so close; she was standing right beside me and her hand, though coarse and rough from the washing-up water, felt light on my forehead.

"Liver attack," she said, but I did not answer. Sunk in a physical torpor, in a marvellous immobility, I felt as if I were floating. I shut my eyes and I would like to have hung a placard round my neck with the inscription: "Please do not disturb."

But Georges came back with the empty salad-bowl and picked up the tray of cheese.

"She asked what was the matter with you," he said, as he brushed by me. "What am I to tell her?"

"*Nothing,*" I said, in English. It was one of the few words that had survived my studies, as if I had learnt English for eight years simply and solely for that word which I brought out now in the most off-hand way.

"Tell her; *nothing.*"

Georges went off with the cheeses and when Hélène learnt what the word meant she was disappointed. She had vaguely hoped it was a swear word.

After luncheon I washed up and I imagined I was a cabin-boy on a wave-tossed boat. About four o'clock I ran into Madame Saulner in the passage.

"But you're frightfully pale!" she exclaimed. "What's the matter with you?"

I faithfully repeated Hélène's diagnosis.

"A liver attack, madame. . . ."

She was almost happy.

" You see how well you eat in my house; the cooking is too rich for you. . . . Restrain yourself in future. . . . One must learn to say ' no,' when one's too fond of eating. . . . And now, go to your room for half an hour and lie down; your face looks quite alarming. . . ."

In my bedroom I was alone with myself and, lying on the bed with my eyes closed, I formulated for the first time that magic phrase: " I think I am going to have a child. . . ."

I did not want my thought to be expressed aloud in the kitchen. I wanted at least a partial liberty for it. I was afraid that this atmosphere of slavery might contaminate the child like moral measles. . . . Suddenly Georges came in. He sat down on the edge of my bed and took my hand in his. I kept silence for some moments; I was not trying to be dramatic but my supposition was so much my own private affair that I hardly dared to share it.

I looked at Georges as if I had never seen him before. He wore his green apron like a schoolboy in disgrace. He did not try to break my silence; he had always liked the security of uncertainty.

" Take off your apron," I told him. And as I raised my head the nausea returned.

" I must go downstairs again. . . ."

" Take off your apron. We've got to talk as if we were free people."

He stared at me, and I said:

193

" I think we're going to have a child. . . ."

" No! " he said, at once proud and terrified. " It's not possible! "

Then he added feverishly, " Are you sure? "

It needed another pillow for me to be able to see his face properly without having to raise my neck which was contracted by the effort to fight down my nausea.

" Yes, I'm almost sure."

He confronted me like a big boy owning up to his first lapse to his mother: " What are you going to do now? . . ."

The question was followed by words that I absolutely refused to listen to. I flung myself against him and pressed my palm against his lips. I could feel his young, unconscious lips like a wound; I did not want him to go on speaking.

" Be quiet . . . oh, *do* be quiet! Or do for once say the words I want you to say. . . ."

He disengaged himself, hostile now.

" You always want me to say the words *you* want. Well, you've only got to dictate. . . . What ought I to say? What *do* you permit me to express? "

I turned my face to the wall and I was ashamed of my tears; I made them disappear into the pillow. It was strange how the tears Georges provoked always humiliated me, as if a stranger had made me cry.

" I love you," he said, from far away. " You *know* that I love you."

194

His limpid voice became more intimate; once again it was tinged with a pride I would never understand; that voice wanted precise details; it wanted to know past and future dates.

But I did not answer; I retired into my unhappiness like a snail retiring into its shell.

Later, when he had gone away again, I sat up. I put my hands on my stomach. It was flat, almost hollow. I felt my narrow hips; under my uniform dress I was abnormally thin. I left the room. This floor was reserved for the maids. They worked late into the evening and now, at five in the afternoon, it was totally silent. My steps echoed as I walked towards the stairs; I continued my way on tiptoe. The spiral staircase seemed narrower than usual. I looked carefully at each step and held on to the banisters which, up till then, I had never used. I went down, turning endlessly round and round; I was no longer frightened. Another feeling had taken possession of me: I was responsible.

What a triumph for Madame Saulner, my leaving her! She did not even allude to our terms of agreement; the opportunity was too splendid! She showered her opinions on me:

" I quite understand, Christine. You're too delicate for this work. . . ."

But she promptly regretted the word delicate; it was too elegant for a servant. She hesitated for a moment, trying to find a more suitable adjective, then said disgustedly:

" You're anæmic . . . I wonder how you'll manage in the future. You haven't even a nationality and French people don't like foreign nursery governesses for their children."

" I've heard the opposite, madame," I said. " There are English girls here. And Swiss girls and Dutch girls and Swedish girls. . . ."

She made a little movement to show her impatience; I could see, from her face, that it was going to be very difficult for her to explain her ideas to me.

" A governess who comes from a country everyone knows is quite a different thing. One can ask for references, one has a minimum of safety for one's children. . . . But you, a Hungarian . . . with your impossible Slavonic language. . . ."

I said mechanically as I always did on these occasions:

" Hungarian is not a Slavonic language, madame. . . . It's a language of the same origin as Finnish. . . ."

She did not like my audacity. She did not like being interrupted and, moreover, I embarrassed her too much with my references to Finland. In her mind all Nordic countries were indistinguishable and she had just had a mental image of Sweden. . . .

I saw that she was drawing towards the end of our conversation. She stumbled over her sentences; she spoke faster and faster like steam raising a saucepan lid higher and higher.

" And that extraordinary notion of yours . . . Writing! "

Under her nervous little laugh I sensed a jealousy that she would never admit to herself.

" Writing . . . whatever next? Building castles in Spain, eh? "

She was as violent as if she had guessed my thoughts. She kept reverting to the word " writing." She savoured it, she wanted to annihilate me, but I remained completely calm. She was so far removed from reality. . . . She did not know of my current manuscript nor of a future one in which I should devote a few pages to her! And, above all, she had no suspicion that I was going to have a child. I could bear anything but I could not have endured her staring at my body; that look of hers that would have travelled down from my breasts to my stomach and stopped at my hips. I could not have borne her playing guessing-games with my life: when, how, why? Passion or carelessness?

I listened to her and I was grateful for that very violence. She fidgeted and twisted about in her chair; she fought so hard to have the satisfaction of seeing me in tears that I was almost sorry for her. What an empty life hers was in which the world was divided into two camps, one filled only with the triumph of the conquerors and the other with the obedience of the conquered.

Finally, she stood up, taller than ever and, with a gesture like that of poor, mad Nero, indicating the blazing ruins of Rome, she pointed to the bookcase.

" You may choose a book as a remembrance. . . ."

She had gone over the borderline and upset the balance of power. Suddenly I was the one who dominated. Thanks to her I was able to reply in a calm voice:

"I do not want any remembrance, madame. I should like to forget you, madame."

# 15

We had not been able to make many social contacts. Nevertheless the miracle happened. One of our few friends lent us the little maid's room that served her as a refuge. She was a newly-fledged mother-in-law and, instead of persecuting her family, she believed herself persecuted by it. I knew her son, a charming, extremely amusing man, and her patient, submissive daughter-in-law. I have never noticed the slightest sign of their being hostile towards her, but, according to my friend, her life was nothing but suffering.

"I'll lend you my room," she said. "But on one condition. As soon as I need it you'll leave within twenty-four hours. Because, you know, I'm on very good terms with them at the moment, but it's only the lull before the storm. And, if my pride is hurt, I retire here at once and wait till they come and implore me to return. The fact is they can't live without me, but it's only my going away that makes them realise how much they need me there."

I consented wholeheartedly to my friend's conditions. Each day was a gift. I would have preferred to know that I had to go on some definite date rather than stay on in this complete uncertainty. I had acquired the habit of breathing deeply; I retained the air in my lungs so as to overcome my incessant desire to vomit. My charming friend did not know I was pregnant and she advanced along the passage with the confidence of those who are blessed with insensitive nostrils. Whereas I . . .

This room was on the ground floor of one of those enormous buildings in Passy that stand along the banks of the grey indifferent Seine. By some odd caprice of the architect it contained a few maids' rooms. The elegant front of the house looked out on a busy square; the severe and useful part was hidden in a little street dominated by doors bearing inscriptions: " Service. Service staircase. Tradesmen." I followed my friend who had entered by one of these back doors; we brushed past some solemn, well-closed dustbins and she drew my attention to the conspicuously placed minute-switch at the right of the entrance. It was dark here, even in daytime, and I was assailed by various odours. I put my handkerchief to my mouth.

She turned to me.

" Have you got a cold? "

I nodded, without speaking.

We went into the dark room that looked out on a tiny square courtyard surrounded by forbidding walls.

" In summer I get a lot of sun here," she affirmed, with as much conviction as if she had wanted to sell me her room. She gently touched the window, saying:

" You see, dear . . . in summer the window is always wide open and I put my plants out of doors. I'm never gloomy here." She opened the window to its full extent and I hastened to lean out of it. It was impossible to glimpse the smallest patch of sky, whether grey or blue.

" And besides," she went on, " it's quiet. I can cry as much as I like here; nobody persecutes me. . . ."

There was a divan with a blue cover, a little table, two chairs and a cupboard. And my friend stood there in the middle of it enraptured, with her grey hair all over the place and her little hat still tipsy from the summer sun that lingered in its yellow felt. The scene was slightly ridiculous; I so longed to be alone and never again to have to utter the words " thank you." Moreover, I would have liked to know where to find the W.C. and water to wash with.

She guessed my thoughts.

" The water, yes, the water. There isn't running water in the room but you've got the tap at the end of another passage that I'll show you . . . and the toilet's down there too. . . ."

Suddenly, I felt very ill and I sat down on the edge of the divan. She settled down happily on a chair and removed her coat, in preparation for a long, intimate conversation. But, suddenly carried away by an idea, she stood up again and hunted for something in the cupboard. She found a spirit-stove. I began to be frightened of the smell.

"Before we have a chat, I'll make you a nice cup of coffee."

She took a bottle from its hiding-place in one of the dark corners and poured a little alcohol into the container.

My stomach turned over in one heave, and, with my handkerchief to my mouth, I plunged into the dark passage in quest of the sinister ill-lit lavatory.

I returned, emptied of all my strength and shivering, with the bitter taste of bile on my tongue.

The little blue flame was flickering under a battered saucepan. My friend looked at me in surprise.

"You did rush off in a hurry! Did you find it?"

Warmed by the coffee, I huddled against a cushion and listened to her without hearing what she said. But, making an effort to come back to reality, I said:

"Georges will be coming soon. . . ."

She turned livid.

"Oh, no. . . . I don't want a man to come into my room!"

I protested feebly:

"A husband's different."

She lowered her voice to explain:

"The neighbours on the right and left don't know that you'll be living here; they're used to seeing me about. . . . I don't want them to get wrong ideas about me; they mustn't hear a man's voice in my room. . . . My reputation . . ."

She added generously:

" But he can help you with carrying the suitcase and the typewriter."

She had managed to find the key word to my existence.

She went on without noticing my thrill of gratitude:

" Because your novel may be good . . . I liked the parts you read to me; you've got talent. . . . And, besides, it's an interesting subject. . . ."

I trembled with delight as I listened to her. It was the first time in my life that someone had taken my work seriously. To hear those magic words! " your novel "; to see her look of conviction! No, she was not laughing at me.

I got up, went over to her and hugged her. She pushed me away, saying:

" Mind my hat! "

But I loved her definitely and for life; I loved her just as she was. I no longer envied her her age and I was no longer unhappy about being young. Perhaps, I told myself, the world lay open before me? She had spoken about my novel . . . my novel. . . .

She went away very late, but I was able to endure that evening. My loneliness was alleviated by hope.

After she had gone I sat alone waiting for Georges. He arrived about nine o'clock, by special permission of Madame Saulner. The cardboard suitcase took its place on a chair like a well-trained old dog that always returns from its wanderings.

" You'll be all right here," said Georges, looking

round the room with as much interest as if he were in a museum.

" Yes. . . ."

Perseveringly I waited for a touch of gentleness. I would like to have seen him at my feet burning with enthusiasm. But, instead of comforting me, he asked the definite question:

" Are you sure? "

" Yes, I'm sure. I've been sick three times. . . ."

" It's incredible," he said, but I saw no sign of wonder at the situation on his face.

" Is your bed comfortable? "

" I don't know. I shall be sleeping in it to-night for the first time."

" True," he said, and added thoughtfully: " You won't be frightened, all alone? "

I wanted to cry with rage. Why did he talk about fear? I had been terrified ever since my friend's departure but, not for anything, would I admit it.

" What's she up to? "

" She " was Madame Saulner.

Georges replied discreetly, as if he were a relative of hers:

" Nothing special, much as usual. . . ."

" And Hélène? "

" In a bad temper. She had to do the washing-up all by herself. I was ironing trousers. . . ."

I was overwhelmed with a sudden tenderness; an acid tenderness. This boy who spoke five languages, who had been destined for a regular career in the Diplomatic Service—Secretary at thirty; Councillor at fifty—had to iron somebody's trousers!

I exclaimed:

" It's appalling this slavery. You really do deserve something better. What idiotic work! "

But he remarked philosophically:

" There's no such thing as an idiotic job. . . ."

We talked for a little while longer, then he went away. I was left alone, in bed, with the little bedside lamp and *Eugénie Grandet* which I was re-reading in French.

Soon, I switched off the lamp, and decided to go to sleep at last. Then, in the pitch-black room, I heard a strange noise, like the twittering of very lively birds. Sometimes I also heard a bang, as if someone had flung themselves against the door. I got up, icy with terror, and examined the door; it was well and truly shut. Now I knew where the noise came from; the birds were twittering outside in the passage. Now and then, after the click of the minute-switch, the birds would be silent. I imagined a thousand frightening possibilities. I no longer dared to move; beads of sweat ran down my neck. I had the feeling that a strange face was looking in at me through the window; it had a flattened nose. Was it Doctor Jekyll or Mr. Hyde? Which of the two was the monster?

I went to sleep with great difficulty, and, the next morning, when I went out into the passage, I saw a little woman in a blue apron who was just closing the door.  She gave me an inquiring look and I replied with a " Good morning, madame."

" Are you living in that room? " she asked.

" Yes, for a few days.  Madame, could you tell me what that noise was all last night, like birds? "

She smiled and said:

" Rats, mademoiselle.  We have a lot of them. . . ."

# 16

THAT VERY MORNING I decided to leave the ground floor and its rats with as little delay as possible and I undertook one of the most difficult tasks imaginable, that of finding a maid's room. All about me the world had changed its familiar face; I hesitated longer before venturing on to a studded crossing and I had to force myself to eat in spite of the profound repulsion I felt for every kind of food. I also wanted to finish my book. I looked on the birth of the child as the frontier of a new life that I must cross with a manuscript in my hand. I was ready to love Georges with a new love fed by this miracle I carried in my body. I wanted to forget all the great and small miseries he had caused me. I looked on love as a sublime duty towards the unknown, towards my child. We had agreed that Georges should stay on with Madame Saulner and that I should find an easier job. We had not so much as adumbrated the word " flat "; that wish would have been quite crazy. But we did talk incessantly about a little room where I could cook without being pursued by an angry hotel proprietor and where, most important of all, I should have a corner for the cradle. I looked at advertisements and my one idea of happiness was to find a few lines that ran: " Wanted, a young couple. Husband to act as secretary; wife to be employed in typewriting."

In that dark little room in Passy I worked fervidly, but the song of the rats had a very demoralising effect on me. I always came in about five o'clock, when it was still light. I pressed the button of the minute-switch and walked down the passage, my heels clattering on the concrete. One Sunday night—I had been living for a week in this handsome building—Georges and I arrived at the entrance. It was ten o'clock—we had been to a little cinema in the neighbourhood—and I wanted to show him the pages I had written during the week. But the minute-switch was no longer working. Despairingly I pressed the little button but with no result. The passage lay before us, drowned in total darkness, as menacing as one of those marshes that swallow up their victim before he has gone three steps.

" I'll never dare to go as far as the room," I whispered, as if I were afraid of being overheard by the rats.

Georges had an ingenious idea.

" If we had a newspaper we could make a torch. . . ."

But where could we find a newspaper? All the kiosks in the neighbourhood shut at eight o'clock. We waited for some other inhabitant of the ground floor to come along, so as to reinforce our caravan a little. But, on a Sunday night, they were all away. We took the métro again and, in the end, we found a newspaper-seller at the Gare Saint-Lazare. An hour later we were back again and Georges lit his torch. Sick with disgust we finally reached the door of my room.

The next day I went off in search of another room. I had decided to ask the concierges in the big expensive blocks of flats, the ones where the lucky tenants were entitled to two or three maids' rooms to a single flat. That foggy morning in February was saturated with the smell of petrol. I walked to the Trocadéro and, on my way, I counted at least six stations where the men, with their big tubes and their meters, were pouring petrol into the avid interiors of cars. I passed them with a handkerchief pressed against my nose, holding my breath, but, though I did not smell the reek, I imagined it and my nausea returned violently.

I crossed the Place du Trocadéro and entered a large block of flats. I was suddenly greatly impressed by the white marble paving of the vestibule and I knocked softly on the glazed door, covered with a yellow silk curtain that was gathered like an eighteenth-century lady's petticoat. A strident voice that contrasted with the sumptuous setting called out:

" What is it ? "

How could I answer in one word through a curtained pane?

" I wanted some information, madame. . . ."

The voice moved about behind the curtain; I could hear it grumbling. Incomprehensible words burst out in a little flood and broke, like waves, inside the lodge.

At last, with a sharp click, a woman opened the door and I saw that she was in process of drying herself. She held a towel in front of her, with which she was both covering herself and dabbing the hollow of her left armpit with her right hand.

I mumbled:

" Madame, is there, by any chance, an unoccupied maid's room in this building? "

Her face expressed such utter incredulity and her shock was so great that she stammered as she replied:

" Wh—what—what . . . a *maid's* room? "

She nearly fainted.

" And you come and disturb me for a crazy thing like that?  It's a disgrace, mademoiselle! "

She banged the door and the shivering panes tinkled with alarm in their yellow petticoats.  I heard one last tart observation:

" These Englishwomen, they're all cracked. . . ."

I could not help smiling as I mentally compared my temporary permit that had to be reauthorised every three months with an English passport that must certainly have a crown on its cover.  At least I hoped there was a crown!

Nevertheless I had the courage to go on because someone had thought I was English.  The second block was just as big but the lodge was plainly visible through the uncurtained pane.  It was like a little stage scene.  A round polished table stood in the middle of the room surrounded by three chairs.

There was an open newspaper and on the opposite wall an enlarged photograph of a smiling young man in uniform. I knocked and a man appeared from an inner room. He stared at me through the glass door and slowly opened it.

" Mademoiselle? "

He had just been drinking his coffee and I recoiled as I smelt his breath.

" Good morning, monsieur . . . I came to ask for some information. Might there perhaps be a maid's room to let in this building? . . . I am a student and . . ."

He shook his head; the door was already closed. He vanished into his kitchen still shaking his head. . . . Perhaps he was dumb?

Going into the third block I ran full-tilt into a severe-looking woman who was preparing to go out shopping with a string bag. I could not see the porter's lodge so I seized the occasion to ask the woman:

" Madame, you don't happen to know where I can find the concierge? "

She replied suspiciously:

" What do you want? *I'm* the concierge."

I was delighted. At last a concierge outside her cage! She would definitely be more amiable, more on a level with human beings. I adopted a polite sophisticated tone:

. " I don't want to keep you, madame; I see you're just going out. . . . You don't, by any chance, happen to know of an unoccupied maid's room in this block of flats?"

Her answer was brief.

"No. Not one."

She opened the large elegant front door and waited for me to pass out in front of her. I hurried away, feeling her gaze planted in the middle of my back.

By midday I was already full of bitterness. As I walked along the street I stared now and then at the huge blocks with all their windows and thought that, in Paris, you had to be born in a flat to get one. But my poor child whom I was expecting would have been only too glad to be born in a properly-heated flat! ... For the moment it was hopeless. By way of lunch I drank a glass of soda-water and ate two rolls. Afterwards I resumed my search. I saw a great many concierges from then on until evening. Nervous concierges, resigned concierges, astonished concierges, angry concierges. Once a woman said to me in a modest little street near the Étoile:

"What a quaint little thing you are, to be sure! Ever so comical. ... Wanting a maid's room ... as if it was as easy as anything!"

Discouraged and mortally tired I returned to the Place du Trocadéro, and, suddenly, I found myself in front of an extremely elegant cemetery. Impelled by a melancholy curiosity, I went in. A conscientious keeper warned me:

"We close in half an hour, mademoiselle. . . ."

I nodded; it seemed perfectly reasonable to me to close a cemetery. My nostrils were full of the stale smell of the wintry fog; it was difficult to breathe.

I sat down in front of a well kept-up mausoleum. I had no thought in my mind; I felt neither morbid nor indifferent. I was drained completely dry by that cruel unproductive day.

I got up slowly, left the cemetery and walked along a quiet little street. "I'll try just once more," I thought, as, clenching my teeth, I noticed a large building. I knocked at the door of the lighted-up lodge; no one answered; I timidly went in. A smiling woman appeared in the doorway of another room, next to the one I was in.

"What do you want, mademoiselle?"

I told her in a dull voice, not at all eager and none too polite, that I was looking for a room.

"Take a seat," she said, and she dusted the chair with her hand.

I thought I must be hearing wrong.

"Take a seat," she repeated, then added:

"There's an empty room on the eighth floor, a very pretty room with velvet curtains and a silk counterpane. And a big wardrobe all decorated with carving. It's well heated because we've got central heating through the building, it's just been installed. ... And then, besides, there's a lovely view, with a real window looking out on the Eiffel Tower. ..."

Taken aback by my silence, she looked at me hard.

"Would that suit you?"

" Yes . . . oh, yes! "

I heard my voice from very far away.

She became more friendly.

" Go up quietly to the first floor; the owners live just opposite the lift. They're ever so nice, especially Madame. But so's Monsieur—I've nothing against him. . . ."

" I think it's too late to-day," I said. " Quarter-past seven. . . ."

She made a face.

" The room's been empty for two days; you'd do better to arrange things straight away. You know, it's very hard to find such a pretty room in Paris. . . ."

I went up to the first floor and I rang the bell. A housekeeper with a gentle, slightly tired face opened the door to me.

" I'd like to speak to Madame."

After a moment's hesitation she showed me into a drawing-room that was furnished both richly and with taste. It was lit by soft, discreet lights concealed behind silk lampshades.

My lucidity returned in this drawing-room bathed in ivory-tinted, artificial light. Here, all the objects had their own life; nothing was brand-new and nothing was shabby. It was a drawing-room where the family had coffee after luncheon, where one straightened a crooked picture with a mechanical little gesture, where a fourteen-year-old adolescent retired now and then to dream. . . .

" Mademoiselle? "

" Madame. . . ."

She had the beauty of a piece of Sèvres porcelain. Tall, slender, dressed in grey, with a jabot of filmy white lace, she advanced towards me. The sly tenacious workings of time, that goes by so fast, were hidden in the velvety half-light and veiled by the kindly lamps. She held out her hand, with its long delicate fingers and her hesitant smile did not destroy the harmony of her face; on the contrary, that smile made her other-worldly beauty friendly, accessible and human.

" Mademoiselle, do sit down. . . . What is it that you want ? "

I was embarrassed by a very distant smell of roast meat that had found its way into the drawing-room through a kitchen door that had been left ajar for a moment. Instinctively I wanted to define that smell, as one searches impatiently for the name of a tune one knows. In a soft voice I began to explain the object of my visit. My words, almost whispered, made little circles in the stillness of the drawing-room, like pebbles thrown into a calm lake.

She must have heard much talk of human misery. I felt myself transformed in her eyes into a living illustration of a theory she must have studied extremely conscientiously. I was the refugee intellectual whom one sees, at first sight, comes from an excellent family. My accent became almost an added charm. The unusual hour of my unexpected visit was pardoned the moment she had reminded herself that misery is entitled to present itself at any time of the day. She questioned me with a great deal of tact. I told her about my departure from Hungary, about my parents in Kufstein, and about my plans, but I did not dare mention the child and I am almost sure I forgot Georges.

Sitting in a patch of pink light, with her sitting opposite me, I did not want to look to right or left. But I was aware of the presence of others. A furtive glance showed me a tall boy with black hair, leaning against the drawing-room door, and the anxious face of the housekeeper hovering mysteriously in another room. She was worried about her dinner.

Suddenly the master of the house made a precipitate entrance. A polite man, whom nothing surprised, he kissed my hand, supposing I was a guest of his wife's, a friend whom he had not met before. But when she explained my " case " to him, he agreed with her at once.

" If that will help you, you can have the room. . . ."

She had not added the word I most dreaded: *provisionally*.

They promised to let me have the key next day, and, as I left, I had the feeling that my poor little winter coat was growing too tight and that this extraordinary piece of good fortune was making me sprout wings.

When I was already in bed listening to the farewell song of the rats who were gaily frisking about in the passage, I remembered something that a furious concierge had said to me: " These women students, what a lot of giddy gadabouts they are! "

I went to sleep, thinking over the day's events and waiting impatiently for the moment when I could tell Georges the great news about the room.

The room on the eighth floor was ravishing and I took possession of it on a sunny day in February. Georges was not in the least amazed by my success and said to me:

" When you want something, you always manage to get it."

This absolute confidence in my strength filled me with apprehension about Georges himself. I was more and more haunted by the idea that I ought to change him. I was waiting impatiently for him to grow up. He had rigid and definite opinions about life. He spoke with great contempt of politics, which had been his family's profession for several generations. Literature bored him, and when I mentioned Baudelaire, he talked about petrol engines and steam engines. I had vaguely heard it said that totally different temperaments understand each other very well because of some mysterious law of attraction; I also had faith in the fact that we were both young. I really and truly wanted to be interested in his affairs, but I had a frantic desire to yawn when he attempted to explain the function of valves or how ball-bearings worked. During the long Sunday afternoons when I lay on the divan, he sat beside me with sheets of paper scribbled over with tiny figures. He added and multiplied at astonishing speed and I had to make a tremendous effort not to close my weary eyelids.

" Is it quite clear to you now ? " he would ask, and I would reply, suppressing an impertinent yawn:

" Yes, it's more or less clear. . . ."

I was afraid of taking away his courage if I admitted that he was boring me to tears, but, one day, when he had explained that our future life depended on the success of one of his inventions, a toy aeroplane, I could not help being anxious.

" It would be much better for you to go all out to try and get a student's grant and go to the University. You'd be an excellent engineer. I've got to work in any case, and in a few years, you'd have a splendid future before you. . . ."

" Do you think so ? " he said dreamily. " Do you really think so ? "

" I'm absolutely sure of it. . . ."

He was so childlike that I suddenly had the feeling that I was Colette's Lea; I was fifty, and he, sitting there beside me, was Chéri.

" I say, darling. . . ."

Hearing him say that word " Chérie " made me start.

He put his hand on my shoulder.

" Don't be so jumpy. . . ."

" What were you going to say ? "

He gave a great stretch, like someone wanting to deliver themselves of a thought.

" I shall go on with my studies in the United States. . . . I shall be an engineer in an atomic centre."

His delicate high-bred face had an expression that worried me. I realised that I had two children; this adolescent dreamer and the one I was carrying.

I heaved a sigh.

He leant over me.

" What are you thinking about? "

He was so rarely concerned about my thoughts that it was an occasion for telling the truth. But I could not see so much as a shadow of uneasiness in those eyes full of frank curiosity, and I did not want to upset him.

" I'm not thinking of anything. . . ."

He smiled radiantly.

" Then I can go on, can I? "

I said, " Yes."

Whereupon he began to explain all over again just how many months it would take, if his invention got going, for us to become millionaires. . . .

# 17

WHEN MY NOVEL was finished I returned to the publishers and the secretary had to make an effort to recognise me. She was completely taken aback by the manuscript I laid on her table and said:

" I'll send you to another publishing firm. . . . I know their Hungarian reader personally."

The publishers to whom she sent me received me kindly and the secretary to whom I spoke assured me that I should shortly receive a letter from her.

I took the métro about six o'clock. The carriage was full and I stood beside a seat on which there were three women. Suddenly one of them stood up.

" Take my seat, madame."

I did not dare protest; I sat down, surprised and embarrassed. I turned my head towards the window and saw the dim reflection of my tired face. Suddenly I knew why she had given up her seat to me. Instinctively, I shifted my right hand towards my stomach and I realised that my winter coat was not buttoned up. Before leaving I had left it open; it was beginning to get too tight for me and I could not move the buttons; they were already on the edge. So people could see that I was expecting a baby. . . . It must be four months old, my child.

As I stepped out of the train I had already made up my mind to go off as soon as possible, to see my parents again; I wanted to feel my mother's warmth. And they knew nothing yet! . . .

Having been unable to obtain a visa for Austria, we decided to get as far as Munich. We hoped that, on the spot, we would be able to obtain a twenty-four hour permit so that I could introduce Georges to my parents. We believed with blind confidence that, after this journey, Georges would find some job that was worthy of him and that would assure our future and that of the child. I was not in the least frightened of the tiring journey; I knew that we should have a long night sitting up in the train, but I was sustained by my longing for this meeting. Now that I was expecting my child, I loved my parents more than ever. I wanted the time to go more quickly: I counted the days and the hours.

Nevertheless, it is extremely difficult to travel when one does not possess the most natural thing in the world: a nationality. It is most difficult of all for a mother-to-be who might give birth anywhere—in the train, in an aeroplane or in the sacred portals of an embassy, and, by that fact, become the stateless mother of a newly-born Frenchman, German or American!

The customs officer stared long and carefully at our travel-permit and everyone in the compartment awaited the outcome with lively interest. I got the impression that, in whichever country I arrived, I should be the extra mouth that would finally let famine loose, the superfluous body that would provoke a housing crisis.

At last he gave us back the apparently inoffensive little book whose scrupulously filled-up pages concealed one of the victims of this day and age, suffering from the worst of contemporary diseases, that of being an émigré.

The night was very hard to bear. My aching body, heavy with the still invisible weight of the miracle inside it, wanted to lie down, but all the seats were occupied. Tormented by a persistent nausea, I left the compartment several times, stumbling over the stiff legs of sleepers in the dim blue light. Out in the corridor, I shivered, but at least I could breathe. Near the door of the lavatory a young soldier lay fast asleep, lying doubled-up, with his head on his knapsack. Like a child. . . .

Suddenly I felt an infinite tenderness for the human beings all round me. It seemed to me that no one could ever be wicked any more and that the entire world was a vast cradle waiting for my child. I wanted to kneel down by that soldier and wake him up with the great news, the marvellous news that my child was going to be born into happiness.

As I pressed my burning face against the damp pane I saw the scenes of my past life unroll before me. But nothing seemed harsh or wounding any more. And, suddenly, I realised that my lips were uttering those magic words, those wise, sweet words that have come down through the ages:

" When God sends a child, He also sends His help."

When we arrived in Munich we learnt that, if we wanted to see my parents, we should have to cross the Austrian frontier illicitly. Austria was still occupied by the four great Powers, and it was they who would have to give us our visas after long months of waiting. I did not want to wait.

Georges and I decided that we would have our marriage regularised religiously and, afterwards, cost what it might, we would try and rejoin my parents.

The idea of a religious marriage filled me with profound alarm. But having been brought up in the strictness of a fervently Catholic family, I wanted to be faithful to tradition.

In Munich we stayed with friends, poor like ourselves, but full of kindness and hospitality. Soon after our arrival I found myself, at eight o'clock in the morning, standing beside a grave and solemn Georges in a little church in Munich. Standing in front of the altar and thinking of the toothless old women muttering their prayers, I had the impression that my back was as broad as a house. Were they going to discover that this early-morning bride was no longer able to button up her coat? Oh, if I only had a really voluminous coat, how well I could have hidden both myself and the child! But, dressed as I was forced to dress, I was exposed to the stares of all and sundry.

We heard Mass on our knees. I was cold, but, on

the prie-dieu, I could not clutch my coat tighter round my body. Yet I did not want the child to catch cold; I was thinking of it and of nothing else.

Lulled by a kind of torpor, as I said my neglected prayers again, it was to my child that I vowed eternal fidelity. . . . As we came out of church I was seized with an irresistible desire to tell the truth; I wanted to tell Georges, that, when I had pronounced the words of the marriage-vow, I had been thinking only of my child. But, when he turned to me and I saw his tender, defenceless face, I kept silent.

With my left hand in his and my right hand clutching my coat, we went off to have breakfast.

The old priest with his gentle, impersonal smile had given us the address of a friend of his who was a parish priest in a little town near the Austrian frontier.

At dawn we took a little local train that deposited us in the rain-drenched village. We crossed the main street and took a little beaten-earth track that ran up the side of the mountain. The village was solidly enclosed in this tiny valley which was probably starved of sun, even in July. We were guided by the plan the priest had drawn on a half-sheet of paper, so that we should not have to inquire our way of the villagers.

I turned to Georges:

" Can you see anything remotely resembling a road in the mountains ? "

He looked about him like the captain of a ship and shook his head.

" I've no idea how the priest will make us cross the frontier. . . ."

Our coats were becoming heavier and heavier with rain and we stopped in front of a well-kept little house, stuck against the steep rise. Georges pulled the string of the little bell fixed beside the door. The sound was stifled almost at once by the rain that came down in torrents. Looking up at the mountain that rose up just behind the house, I saw a foaming river pouring down from the heights and rushing furiously towards the valley.

The door opened abruptly but the grey-haired woman who stood in the doorway had nothing hostile about her; she merely seemed extremely surprised at our intrusion.

" Could we speak to His Reverence? " Georges asked, and his impeccable German dissipated the housekeeper's uneasiness.

Without taking off our coats we went into a dining-room where a table was laid for breakfast and a fat earthenware coffee-pot gave out a friendly welcoming smell.

" Sit down," said the housekeeper. " The Father has just finished saying his Mass. He'll be back in a few minutes to have his breakfast."

" I'm terribly hungry," I muttered in Georges's ear, and the big country loaf and the fresh butter looked more and more appetising every second.

The priest arrived and welcomed us very kindly, especially when he heard that we had been sent to him by his best friend. Without inquiring the reason for our visit, he rang the little bronze bell that stood by his plate. When the housekeeper appeared, he asked her to bring two more cups and said we must have some coffee with him.

It was a long time since I had eaten with such appetite. As we ate, we explained our project to him.

The priest promptly became very uneasy.

"The frontier is near," he said, "but I don't at all like risking a business like this. Go back to Munich and wait quietly for your visa."

I was seized with a vast despair. I turned to him so as to catch his faded blue eye.

"Father, I'm expecting a child; I must see my parents before it is born."

He stared at me with astounded eyes.

"You want to cross the frontier on foot when you're expecting a child?"

I absolutely had to persuade him.

"I implore you. Truly, truly, I can still walk very well. The priest in Munich told us it was only ten kilometres. We'll walk slowly but I *must* see my parents again. I shan't have a moment's peace if I can't see them again. . . ."

And I added, as a reference, as a final recommendation:

"I did thirty-five kilometres with my parents when we had to cross the Austro-Hungarian frontier. It's true I wasn't expecting a child, but it was quite an ordeal, all the same. . . ."

The priest's delicate face, further refined by the nobility of age, softened again.

"What hardship! Poor, cruelly-tried generation...."

I was profoundly struck by those words that came back to me from the past like an exact echo—a distant echo, but clear and sorrowful. Monsieur Radnai in the cellar.... During that infernal siege.... When he looked at me his eyes were misty with a strange tenderness; he was one of those persecuted men who are terrified by the world's savagery but who no longer think of themselves but of the young who would have liked to live.... "Poor generation," he used to say during the bombardment.... I was fifteen, and, at the time, those words had filled me with an extraordinary pride; an immeasurable pride that had annihilated fear. It was as if he had dubbed me knight ... knight of that capricious fate that made grass grow between the outspread fingers of the corpses that peopled the lunar streets of Budapest....

"Christine ... Christine...."

Georges's insistent voice brought me back to reality.

"Are you feeling ill?" the priest inquired anxiously.

"Oh, no, thank you. I was only thinking...."

Georges whispered a well-worn schoolboy joke to me in Hungarian. He had an inexhaustible repertory of them.

"You always turn pale when you think, it's the tremendous unaccustomed effort...."

The priest stood up.

" My children, the important thing is that you shouldn't be seen climbing the mountains."

He threw me an anxious glance; he had frightened himself by uttering that word " mountain." I straightened my back, and, with a great sigh, I pulled in my stomach to show him how slim and athletic I was, ready to face up to this insignificant little stroll.

In the hall he picked up his black overcoat and his umbrella and called out:

" Madame Hilda! "

She appeared.

" I'll be back in an hour."

As we went out we walked round to the back of the house, then through the garden. After a few minutes' walk through the deluge, we passed through the iron gate that marked the end of his domain, and found ourselves on the steep mountain slope strewn with pine-needles and rotting leaves.

We walked in Indian file. His black umbrella bobbed among the trees like a mushroom swelled to giant size by the wet. The water squelched softly in my shoes and I held on to Georges's hand: he was walking between me and the priest.

Suddenly the curtain of rain thinned and I had the sensation that the inhabitants of the village were looking out of their windows and watching us attentively. We were so alarmingly visible; big black ants climbing awkwardly up in the wake of a black umbrella.

When we were on the crest of the mountain it stopped raining. At the bottom of the descent before us stretched a vast meadow; farther away, covered with mist, we could dimly see a farm. We could even make out some cows, tiny as drops of water.

" Don't be frightened when you get to the farm," the priest told us. " The people who live there are good-hearted. . . . Near the house you'll find a road that will lead you into a little forest. You'll also see a chapel where I say Mass every other Sunday, and, after that chapel, you'll come to the main road, a concrete road. That's already Austria. Follow it and you'll find a village where you can get a train that takes you to Kufstein."

He went off hurriedly without waiting for us to thank him, and soon he had disappeared behind the trees.

Thus, we found ourselves alone, on the edge of an unknown world, committed to cross an invisible frontier that separated two countries.

" Come along," said Georges, and we plunged into the tall, soaking grass that froze my legs. But why should the cold do me any harm on the road that was leading me to my parents?

I was transported by the uplifting idea of accomplishing a great feat. I looked ahead of my feet. I did not want to stumble unnecessarily. I was thinking of my child whose first journey this was.

Exhausted and mortally weary, we arrived on the outskirts of the farm. The cows had resumed their normal size; they stared at us with mild complacency as we walked into the farm kitchen.

When the farmer's wife heard that we had been sent by the parish priest, she put two bowls of milk, still warm from the cow, on the table and two big hunks of bread. She would not accept the money Georges offered her and her tall daughter, with her plaits wound round her head, accompanied us as far as the little chapel. When we were on the main road, in Austria at last, I began to shake all over.

" Just a little more courage, and we'll be at the station," Georges told me.

But I could only see a village as far away as the farm had been when we had seen it from the summit.

I walked like an automaton and the sun no longer traced more than a faint yellow streak on the fields. Georges looked at his watch.

" It's half-past four," he said.

We had left the village about half-past eight.

I would like to have talked to Georges, to have expressed the thoughts that haunted me, but he profoundly loathed my touching on our feelings towards each other. He would almost have preferred a bombardment to an analysis. All the same I would have liked to tell him that, in spite of his closed, hermetically sealed mind, we had never felt ourselves so much at one as during that crazy walk.

" Georges? "

I had spoken his name aloud in spite of myself.

" Are you very tired? " he replied.

" Yes, but that doesn't matter in the least. . . . I'd like to tell you that . . ."

I silently implored him: " Help me . . . we have a unique, marvellous chance to find each other. . . ."

But he noticed nothing whatever. . . .

By the time we reached the station, I was no longer walking, I was just dragging myself along.

The compartment was empty; I was able to lie down on one of the seats.

I shut my eyes and thought that our marriage was a true marriage, not like the ones I had seen contracted at the French Legation in Budapest in 1945 . . . so as to be able to leave the country with a passport! . . . But I did not want to remind myself of all those old stories. One day, perhaps, I may tell them. . . .

Georges woke me up at Kufstein.

I found the little station just as I had left it, with all my hopes, a year ago. It was dark when we arrived at the hut where my parents lived. There was a light in their window. I made a sign to Georges and we looked in at my parents sitting quietly at a table. The room had changed its appearance. I saw books everywhere; my father was reading and my mother was mending a shirt. Although I was exhausted I still lingered outside; I was afraid to disturb their apparent peace, even with a joy.

When we knocked at the door my mother opened it. For some minutes she stood there, quite stunned at the sight of us.

How lovely that evening was! I was happy and I found once again a security that I had so terribly lacked. My parents were very sweet to Georges. They embraced him as if he were a son who had returned from a distant journey. When my parents learnt that I was expecting a baby and that we had crossed the frontier illicitly, they could find no words to say.

Mamma put me to bed and heaped me up with pillows. I had my dinner in bed. I wanted to laugh and cry with happiness. How I loved my parents! And, thanks to them, I was going to be a little girl again, even if only for two days. . . .

Our arrival caused a sensation in the camp, and, at the end of the second day, the Commandant sent a man to warn us that he wanted to see our papers the following morning. A submarine that has long been lying motionless in the depths of the sea does not welcome divers who come from another world. And we had returned from another world. We were obliged to leave the next morning at dawn and to go back the way we came. My father accompanied us through the fields as far as the frontier. It was a heartrending good-bye. That day I made a vow to myself that I would do everything I could to have them with me for life.

Before taking the train from Munich back to Paris,

I followed my mother's advice and went to see a doctor. When he had examined me, he said:

"You are very narrow in the hips, madame. . . . It's extremely likely you may have complications. . . . You must take great care of yourself. . . . You must have a good doctor. . . ."

We took the train back to Paris that very night.

# 18

IN PARIS we went back to the little room that was our one and only refuge and Georges did the impossible to find some work. He presented himself everywhere that the advertisements announced someone wanted a capable young man. During the first days after our return, I waited for him, lying on the divan with a book bought for a few francs from a second-hand bookstall. I read from morning till night, but I had only to raise my head to be seized with a nausea that obliged me to run the whole length of the corridor to reach the lavatory. I was hungry, with an impetuous, arrogant hunger that was difficult to appease. But we had so very little money that I did not dare so much as venture into those elegant shops that surrounded the block of flats. I went down with Georges into the busy Rue de Passy and there, for fifty francs, we bought oil, a salad, a few potatoes and, very occasionally, a little rib of pork. But, during the long afternoons, I would imagine tables exquisitely laid, with flowers scattered on an embroidered cloth and candles shedding soft golden light on the heavy silver. And, on this elegant table, I served all sorts of Lucullan menus. Before our departure to Germany we had still been able to buy quarter-bottles of soda-water that marvellously subdued my nausea but, since our return, this had become too great a luxury.

When, by exceptional luck, I felt a little better, I used to go and sit at the window during Georges's absence and look at the roofs of Paris. The spring was still too young and twilight fell fast and early, but there were moments when the roofs were flooded with pink light and when the Eiffel Tower looked like a child's drawing done with a heavy, blunt pencil. How far away Paris seemed from that window! I was tortured by the idea that I was going to die when my child was born. In the four months of life that remained to me, I wanted to write another novel. But I lacked the physical strength; my back was too painful and I was hungry all the time. Georges arrived towards evening. I was full of cares and anxieties but what could I have told that boy who came in pale and exhausted, not knowing where to turn next? I was convinced that my future life, if I survived, would be merely a dreary vegetating, with ideas cut off at the root and resentments one could not even express.

When the child kicked me during the night I seemed to feel its sharp, impertinent little toe; in the darkness, I kept saying ardently to myself: " I want you to be strong; I want you to be *very* strong. . . ."

I shall never be able to define my behaviour towards Georges. At what precise moment did I

236

begin to keep silent? I was probably the egoist who does not like being unhappy or the vain woman who will never admit defeat. I wanted, with a morbid obstinacy, to preserve the appearances of happiness and, when I looked at Georges asleep—he slept on a mattress on the floor beside my bed—I felt responsible for him. I had now got into the habit of tidying up after him, as if I had replaced the nurse of his childhood, and, to comfort myself, I had to have recourse to well-worn phrases such as: " Men will always be children."

But, when I looked at the Eiffel Tower, I never stopped thinking of our expedition, already long ago now, and that monster of iron lacework filled me with horror and admiration.

Our hopes of a peaceful future rested on a very slender foundation. One of our Hungarian friends was attempting the apparently impossible so that we could settle in Belgium. I felt a dull lump of misery inside me at the thought of our being forced to leave France in order to be able to live and I knew that the real France, the kind, welcoming France had not yet shown us her face. I sometimes wanted to cry out: " France, I'm here, I love you! I was brought up admiring you; I want to write French books; I want you to be my other native country. Great France, marvellous France, why don't you want to know that I am here? "

The roofs and the grey smoke that wreathed up into the impassive sky did not answer me.

In the old days, I had never thought that one could suffer from hunger and look covetously at a grocer's shop window. Not far from us, there was a dairy, and the good woman, who always wore a white overall, one day hung up a bunch of bananas in her window. At first the bananas were almost green and the bunch intact, but what contemptuous, almost cruel arrogance in their exorbitant price! Each day they grew yellower and yellower. Sometimes, when I hurried very fast past her shop, I saw the dairywoman cut off four or five of them with an enormous knife. I would have really loved to eat one.

Georges came home one night with excellent news. He had found a job. A Hungarian carpenter, long settled in France, wanted his French wife to learn Hungarian. So he had engaged Georges to give his wife an hour's lesson every day at two hundred francs a time. The only snag was that they lived near the Invalides and we lived in the neighbourhood of Passy. The daily métro ticket would have taken a cruel slice off his fees. Georges decided to go on foot. The next day I went with him for the first lesson. We had constantly been told that, if a pregnant woman walks a great deal, the birth will be easy.

While Georges was giving his lesson I sat meekly in the workshop on a stool. I breathed deeply so as to be able to endure the smell of glue that assailed me like little waves breaking against a rock.

The carpenter, ankle-deep in wood-shavings, said to me from time to time:

" All right, madame?" Then he bent lovingly over his plane. He spoke to me in laconic little sentences, without waiting for my reply, and I found this one-sided conversation profoundly restful. " Because that's how life is, madame," he said. " Love. After love comes the child, and worries and little bits of happiness, too. You've got a young husband, he'll make his way. But it's not funny, being far from one's own country. . . . Me, I've been here twenty years. I fought in the war with them. I've got French nationality; my wife's French; my children are French. They don't know a word of Hungarian. What d'you expect? They speak their mother's language, it's only natural. . . . You see, I haven't got the time. . . . I'm from Szeged. . . . Ah, so you know Szeged? Beautiful city . . . so's Budapest. . . . My mother died two years ago. . . . She never understood how one could live with anyone who wasn't Hungarian. . . . She was a very brave woman, my mother—eight children . . . and two miscarriages. . . . I'm not saying this to frighten you, but it's not easy, giving birth. . . ."

Here I was overwhelmed by a feeling of peaceful eternity, a third-class eternity, simple and kindly. It was warm: there were murmurs from the neighbouring room; an occasional customer would come in, more to chat than to order some work. But the carpenter did not interrupt his own task and I watched him with admiration. This was a man who had a bedroom, a table, plates and all the food he needed.

239

Here, I had an unbearable desire to have a tiny lodging, a wardrobe with at least two dresses in it and a big, warm, loose coat. Where was my child going to be born? What bed would I be in ... and what country?

After the lesson the cabinet-maker's wife gave us some really hot coffee and that friendly drink gave me an incredible sensation of well-being. They thought that Georges gave lessons all day; they never suspected that the two of us and the child subsisted on their daily two hundred francs. But, afterwards, about seven o'clock, we had to go out and walk back uphill to Place du Trocadéro. On those return journeys, the city seemed vast and the streets endless. Hanging on Georges's arm, I walked conscientiously, with small, even steps; I did not want to jolt my child.

" You'll give birth to it just like dropping a letter in the letter-box. . . ."

I did not like comparisons of this kind; without my knowing why, they humiliated me a little. But, I replied, with false gaiety:

" Yes, of course. . . ."

All the same, in the depths of myself, I was preparing myself for a tragedy. Involuntarily, I lived through a thousand imaginary death-beds. I saw Georges a widower, with a new wife who would have a pony-tail and flat heels. He often told me he would like me to wear my hair like that and he regarded my high heels with ill-disguised hostility. I have never been able to understand his crazy passion for youth: he was so young himself. . . . For him, anyone over thirty was already middle-aged and, if it were a woman, it was better not to mention her. . . . A woman of thirty! . . . That was something ridiculous! . . . He had told me once that I still had seven years left in which to wear bright-coloured dresses because, after thirty, one had to be careful. Without expressing the thought, I felt in my bones that I should leave him before that fatal birthday. But I knew, too, that I should make a superhuman effort not to die in giving birth. I wanted to bring up my child myself.

Georges went off to sleep quickly at night and I imagined touching or grotesque scenes that made me smile or cry in the dark. I saw Georges at my funeral in a top-hat and a morning coat and I shivered when I thought of him saying to my child: " Oh, your Mamma was very nice; she was fond of writing; one day, I can't imagine why, she cut off her long fair hair." And I also saw my photograph covered with dust. . . . After visions of this sort, I sat up in the narrow little bed and I clasped my hands over my stomach so that the child should not feel my useless emotion. I loved my child with a wild passion and, when I was very hungry during the night, I consoled myself by thinking of the wisdom of nature; I knew that the child was nourishing itself on my blood and my heart. I was aware of its presence with a feverish joy, full of excitement and apprehension. The absolute poverty in which we lived filled me with a blind trust in God. I awaited his miracle with the steadfastness of those who are no longer anxious for themselves but who want to create a new world for their children.

Once, when I was going to the carpenter's with Georges, I was seized with a violent attack of nausea. The world swam dizzily round me, and, leaning against the wall of a house, with my handkerchief clutched against my mouth, I told Georges I could not stay sitting up on a chair for an hour; I simply must lie down. He could not come back with me; the lost lesson would have meant our having to go without food. I allowed myself the luxury of a métro ticket and returned home alone. The journey seemed interminable; I kept my handkerchief against my face the whole time. Opposite me a man who was reading his paper gave me a glance from time to time that said very plainly that sick women ought to remain at home.

I ran, stumbling, all the way from the métro station to the block of· flats. I was trembling as I passed through the glass door and I barely said thank you to the smiling concierge, all set for a chat, for the letter she handed me and which I put in my worn little handbag. I crossed the courtyard to go up the back way, but the lift was stuck somewhere higher up and I had to climb all the stairs to the eighth floor. When I reached it at last, I fumbled in my handbag for my key; alas, Georges had it in his pocket. The little door looked to me as high and inexorable as Mont

Blanc. Seized with an uncontrollable giddiness and nausea, I had to go to the lavatory. There, I sat down on the tiled floor and burst into tears. Later, I went back to my door; my next door neighbour, hitherto invisible, was standing in her doorway.

" Are you ill, madame? "

" Yes, I am ill . . . and I can't get in; I've forgotten the key."

" Come into my place," she said.

She took me over to her window and opened it.

" You see, there's a concrete ledge," she said. " And, below that, there's a little zinc platform. You could climb along to the window of your room, if it's open. . . ."

Shaking all over, I answered that it might be open.

With the help of the neighbour, I climbed on to a chair and found myself outside on the ledge. She had hold of my hand.

" Don't be frightened and, whatever you do, don't look down! "

I clutched her hand tight but eventually I had to let go of it and, all alone, I did the four steps that separated me from our window, that was luckily half-open.

" Yes, I can get in," I called out and, two seconds later, I was in our room.

Opening the front door, I said thank you to my neighbour out in the passage. And then, I collapsed on the divan without an ounce of strength left in me.

The eight stories, the walk along the ledge, my violent sickness and my utter exhaustion sent me to sleep almost at once. As I drifted into unconsciousness, I heard someone, very far away, muttering the cruel words: " It is not so easy to live." But the person was myself.

# 19

THE LETTER I received that day was from the Hungarian reader. He had read the manuscript of *Wanda* and wanted to talk to me about it. I rang his telephone number and a man's voice, a pleasant, friendly voice, answered me. He invited me to come and see him. Later on, in the afternoon, I realised that he had been a successful author in Budapest and that one of his plays had been acted all over the world. I remembered that my parents had often spoken of him; Mamma had once described him as a young man with black hair who had been married successively to the three greatest actresses in Hungary.

We made an appointment for the following morning and there was no possibility of making myself even a tiny bit pretty. My heavy, clumsy shape was even more apparent in my ridiculous coat; I had no lipstick and I had had to do my hair in a little bun, which I hated, to disguise its length.

The block of flats where he lived was a luxurious one; red carpet on the stairs; a lift; a well-polished bell beside the imposing door of the flat. I rang: a maid opened the door.

" Madame ? "

" I want to speak to Monsieur Gindy."

" You have an appointment ? "

" Yes."

" Wait a moment, if you please."

She disappeared, and I was extremely impressed. So one could live in exile and not be poor!

The maid reappeared with a more reassuring face and showed me into a large, luxuriously-furnished room where a white-haired gentleman, with a face furrowed with wrinkles, rose from his arm-chair to greet me.

" Mademoiselle," he said, in Hungarian, and he added, in an almost frightened way: " But you're appallingly young! . . . Do sit down."

I took a chair and looked at him with undisguised curiosity.

He was tall and elegant and he wore a silk dressing-gown. The remains of breakfast on a silver tray looked like a sumptuous still-life in the background. Clumsily, I tried to say that I had imagined him younger, when his face was suddenly lit up by a smile. And that gay, unaffected, boyish smile effectively restored his youth.

He took a cigarette and I reached mechanically for my handkerchief; I could not endure the smell of tobacco.

" And *I* was expecting to see a *femme fatale* this morning! " he said. " The author of *Wanda*, with her numerous lovers! And I see a thin little girl, indecently young."

He had not noticed that I was pregnant. This brilliant man, accustomed to extraordinary women who queened it on the stage, had never had a child.

" How old are you ? "

" Twenty-two. . . . Have you read my novel ? "

" But of course I've read it . . . and I think it's very good."

The room seemed to be revolving round me and I heard his voice:

" Are you ill ? "

" No, I'm happy. You know, I was so longing to hear you say that."

" I've told the publisher he ought to get it translated," Monsieur Gindy went on.

I interrupted him excitedly:

" I'm going to write another one soon."

He made a gesture with his big, white, ringless hand to calm me.

" Not so fast: the problem of publishing is a very difficult one. . . . Don't forget there's always a publishing crisis on when a young author turns up. . . . But I have confidence in you," he added, with a charming smile.

And suddenly, seized with a man's curiosity, he leant towards me and asked me, in an intimate voice that demanded a sincere answer:

" What gave you the idea of writing that story."

I explained volubly, completely forgetting the smoke of his cigarette:

" Monsieur Gindy, I once saw a woman who was

like my heroine, but I've invented innumerable things. . . ."

We talked for half an hour, and, for me, it was like the beginning of a new life. A well-known man, an established writer believed in me! Before I left, he gave me one of his books that had appeared in French, and wrote an inscription in it:

" To a young colleague, with every friendly wish from Gindy."

By the word " colleague," he had consecrated me a writer.

During the following weeks I saw him several times and our friendship developed smoothly and naturally. I told him how much I admired his not being poor like all the other Hungarians I knew. He was suddenly taken aback.

" Goodness, don't think this place is my own. I rent one of the rooms in the flat and they bring me my breakfast; they know I never get up before ten. They're charming people, but don't imagine that life's easy for me."

His uneasy glance came to rest on an extraordinary picture.

The picture showed, from the back, a slender, naked young woman with translucent flesh, her profile turned towards a mysterious landscape. Over her left shoulder, hiding the soft curve of one breast, floated a tiny muslin scarf. The picture was exquisitely evocative; it was the living presence of a woman, of the eternal woman. . . .

" Even if I were starving, I wouldn't sell it,"
Monsieur Gindy frequently said. And, when he said
it, the childish shoulders of the frail beauty seemed to
become the very symbol of love.

He did not often speak of his famous wives. He
had lived so close to them, for so many years, that he
had not found them as extraordinary as all that.

I told him that I was married and, once, I took
Georges to see him. I was still waiting for a definite
answer from the publisher.

" I'm going to write my next books in French," I
told Monsieur Gindy. He replied:

" You're still very young; no doubt you'll really
manage to do it. . . ."

He never knew that we were wrestling with troubles
of the most menacing kind.

One day I saw that his picture had disappeared.
That day he was mortally pale and I did not dare ask
a superfluous question. When I left, he said:

" Poor little future French writer. . . . And you're
expecting a child. . . ."

We held hands longer than usual at parting. But
he was looking at the empty space where his picture
had hung on the wall.

Good luck arrived in the form of a brief letter posted
in Belgium. Our faithful friend had not forgotten
us. He wrote, sending us the money for the journey,
and saying that his Belgian friends had been touched
by our plight, and that we were invited to stay in a

château. A job was already in sight for Georges and a layette had been prepared for the child.

It did not take long to pack the cardboard suitcase! I returned the key of our room and I warmly thanked the people who had given it to us. On the day of our departure, I learnt that an ambulance had just removed the concierge to a lunatic asylum.

" Apparently she's mad," said the people on our floor.

It wrung my heart. I did not know whether the kind concierge's madness lay in loving human beings who rebuff every friendly feeling or whether she had gone mad on account of those very human beings around her. But I shall always remember her face and those words she uttered: " There's a very pretty room, mademoiselle. . . . It's empty. . . ."

In the train, I said to Georges:

" My child is going to be born in security."

He stifled a little laugh, as if I had made some schoolboy joke.

" You always say ' *my* child '. . . ."

I turned scarlet and, the first time I crossed a frontier legally, I crossed it with my teeth clenched.

# 20

EVER SINCE the morning I had been lying motionless on that bed. The walls were light blue, and, in the right-hand corner, there was a china statue of the Virgin. On the bedside table, lay the book I had been reading last night: it was the last volume of *Les Thibault* that I wanted to re-read in French. That morning I had been gripped by a new, deep pain I had never known before. Georges had already gone to his office; it was his second day at work. They told me he would come and see me between one and two. Beside me, on the left, was a little empty white bed. It was the bed of my child who was soon going to be born. When a wave of pain broke over me, I gripped the white-painted iron bars. That little empty bed helped me enormously. From time to time, a silent nun entered and walked up to my bedside. I tried not to see her face; I looked up at the white ceiling; I did not want to be disturbed in my suffering.

I was thirsty and, during the rare moments of respite, I moistened my lips with iced water. Georges's pale face appeared; he wanted to talk to me, but I turned my face towards the little bed and did not answer. I wanted to be alone with my child. This birth was a personal affair between the two of us.

We were accomplices in the act of creation. No one and nothing must come near its little bed.

Twilight fell. The doctors' incessant bustling to and fro annoyed me. They were there all the time, asking me pointless questions and being surprised that I did not scream. The extravagant pain kept attacking me, cutting me in two; often it left me without any breath. But, through this crazy suffering, the child would belong to me and me alone. A nun told me that Georges was outside in the corridor. The number of doctors increased; at certain moments there were five of them round my bed. When they wiped the sweat off my face, I asked for some information. I wanted to know the exact time. Eleven o'clock at night.

Suddenly there was more bustle than ever in my room. Two nurses pushed in a trolley and laid me on it as if on a stretcher. We trundled very fast along the corridor. Everywhere, outside the doors, I saw vases of flowers. It was hot, and deft hands were pushing me towards an unknown destination. The operating theatre was full of blinding light and, in the multiple mirrors of the projectors, I could see myself lying prone. A young doctor bent over me and the very moment I felt the needle in my arm, I fell into unconsciousness.

Suddenly, I heard a voice repeating over and over again: " Where's my child? ... Where's my child? . . . ."

The face of a nurse, enlarged out of all proportion,

was right in front of my eyes. She was not saying anything. Who, then, was asking: " Where is my child ? "

" You're going to see her soon," she answered at last. So it really was I who was speaking.

I thought that grey light must be the morning.

With a tremendous effort I turned my head and saw Georges sleeping peacefully in an arm-chair. I called to him. He did not hear.

A nurse came in with a swaddled bundle in her arms. She held the bundle out to me. My child was asleep. Her skin was pink and transparent.

" It's a lovely little girl, madame," the nurse told me.

I did not hear anything more.

I was obliged to wake up from that lethargic sleep because the doctor was slapping my face. Everybody wanted me to wake up but I had an irresistible desire to abandon myself to sleep once more.

My body was one mass of pain. And I thought of all the pains that were awaiting me.

I told the nurse in a hoarse voice that I would like to feed my child.

" Madame, one never has any milk after a cæsarean, especially when it was such a serious one."

She knew nothing about life, that nurse. She thought I was going to be satisfied with a rule or a principle. I wanted to feed my child so I *must* have some milk.

My daughter was beside me in her little bed. She

was asleep, and I had not the strength to hold out my hand to her. But I looked at her; my life was anchored in her pink, peaceful face.

Later on I thought about flowers. I must have flowers in my room like the others; I did not want the nurses to say that. . . .

" Georges ? "

" Yes ? "

He came up close to me.

" Would you bring me some flowers ? "

" Yes, I'll bring you some flowers. . . ."

Holding the door ajar, he said:

" What kind of flowers do you want? "

I was too weak to know which month we were in. I tried to think, but I could not.

I repeated obstinately:

" Bring me some flowers. . . ."

I wanted to be alone with my child. In the little room, there were only the two of us now; she and I. Suddenly she began to cry. It was the first time. And it was to me she was crying. My beloved daughter. . . .

Georges came back with the flowers. I stared at him as if he were a stranger. I did not understand what he was doing in this room. That night had separated me from him.

During the days that followed, I was in pain. Pain was my entire occupation. I could neither eat nor drink, and an absent-minded nurse, a novice in discretion, told me that I had nearly died.

Lightning Source UK Ltd.
Milton Keynes UK
UKHW020209011220
374377UK00006B/1377